This edition
has been limited to
2,500 numbered copies
of which this is
No. *201*

To Graham
very best Wishes
Alan Ham

Legends of the
Somerset & Dorset Railway

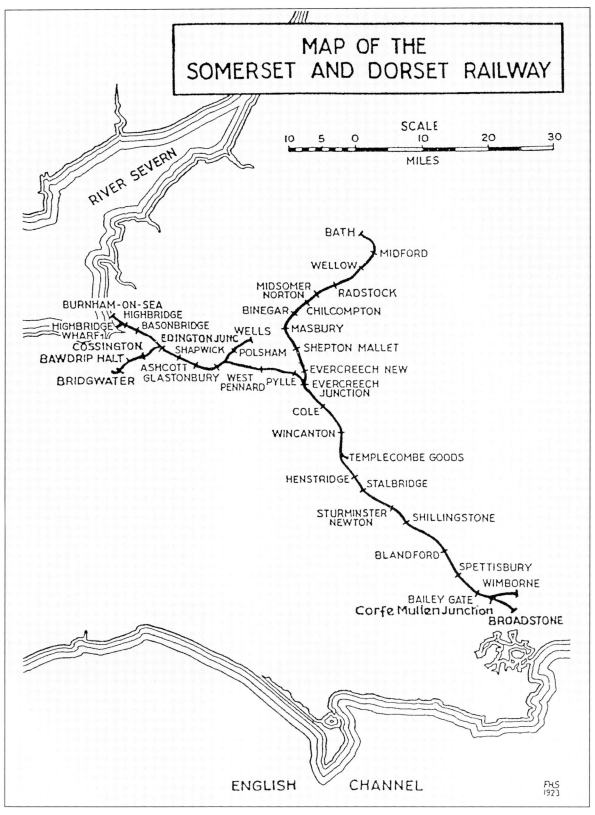

MAP OF THE
SOMERSET AND DORSET RAILWAY

SCALE

10　5　0　　10　　　20　　　30

MILES

RIVER SEVERN

BATH
MIDFORD
WELLOW
MIDSOMER
NORTON
RADSTOCK
BINEGAR
CHILCOMPTON
BURNHAM-ON-SEA
HIGHBRIDGE
HIGHBRIDGE
BASONBRIDGE
WELLS
MASBURY
WHARF
EDINGTON JUNC
COSSINGTON
SHAPWICK
POLSHAM
SHEPTON MALLET
BAWDRIP HALT
ASHCOTT
EVERCREECH NEW
BRIDGWATER
GLASTONBURY
WEST
PENNARD
PYLLE
EVERCREECH
JUNCTION
COLE
WINCANTON
TEMPLECOMBE GOODS
HENSTRIDGE
STALBRIDGE
STURMINSTER
NEWTON
SHILLINGSTONE
BLANDFORD
SPETTISBURY
WIMBORNE
BAILEY GATE
Corfe Mullen Junction
BROADSTONE

ENGLISH　CHANNEL

FHS
1923

This 1923 map of the Somerset & Dorset Railway shows all stations except the halts of Stourpaine & Durweston, Charlton Marshall, Corfe Mullen, which all opened in 1928, and Shoscombe & Single Hill, which opened in 1929. (*by courtesy of the Somerset & Dorset Railway Trust*)

Legends of the
Somerset & Dorset Railway

Alan Hammond

Millstream Books

This book is dedicated to Cliff Smith who passed away on 6 March 2004

Cliff was a great friend of mine who worked on the Somerset & Dorset Railway as a fireman. Over the years that I knew him, he gave me a great amount of help, advice and encouragement with my S&D books. He loved his railways and had a wealth of knowledge that he shared with many others. He always had a smile on his face and nothing was too much trouble. Cliff really was a lovely man who will be greatly missed by many who came into contact with him. He was a Railway Legend in his own right.

First published in 2005 by
Millstream Books, 18 The Tyning, Bath BA2 6AL

Set in Times New Roman and printed in Great Britain by
The Amadeus Press, Cleckheaton, West Yorkshire

© Alan Hammond 2005

ISBN 0 948975 72 5

British Library Cataloguing-in-Publication Data:
a catalogue record for this book is available from the British Library

Foreword

My associations with railways are a little tenuous, steam railways even more so. And yet like a lot of people born in the 1950s, I have nostalgia and a feeling of romance for that era.

My dad used to take me to Willesden rail yards to see the great puffing engines and the endless coal trucks. They were gigantic to a small lad, and were quite scary to witness close up. Sometimes I'd wait on a bridge and stand over the lines, just to see what a face full of steam felt like – my excuse is that I was young! When I lived in Guildford, I paid homage to the Bluebell Line a few times, and had a close up tour of the big engines in their sheds. It might sound obvious but these beauties were enormous standing next to them.

Then in 1987 playing the role of 'Buster' Edwards, one of the Great Train Robbers, I finally came the closest I'd ever come to something so powerful as to give you nightmares; albeit a diesel and not the subject of this book. However the moment is worth savouring, if only to justify the envy and awe we give the railways of yesterday. When filming the robbery itself, I had to crouch beside the line and wait for the famous engine to grind to a halt by my head at ground level, fooled by the green light being changed by the gang to a red. The sheer size and weight of this beast looming over me was very memorable!

I suppose all this had some kind of effect on me because just after 'Buster' I decided to start a model railway in my basement. It was a mish mash of traditional English stock and American stock – a specialist's nightmare – but it was a pretty spectacular layout of which I was very proud.

Anyway, one way or the other, I've been a fan of railways since I was very young and that qualifies me, it seems, to write a foreword to this book by Alan Hammond. He loves railways, I love railways – presumably if you've bought this book, you love railways. So, forget how many rivets this or that engine had, or whether the 1949 Bullnose was more efficient than the 1952 version in the standard livery. Just as my enthusiasm is fuelled by the affection I have for the golden era of steam, when villages had shops not hypermarkets, you could count the cars on the road and when you went to get petrol, a friendly man came and helped you, in short life was simpler. I would imagine your enthusiasm is fuelled by similar things.

Why not browse through these pages of *Legends of the Somerset & Dorset Railway* and remember, it might be the closest you'll ever get.

Phil Collins, 2005

5

Introduction & Acknowledgements

What is long past is cherished most. This for many is the Somerset & Dorset Railway. It seems like only yesterday when the Pines Express ran from Bath to Bournemouth or when the local branch goods train, affectionately known as the Highbridge Market, trundled across the misty Somerset levels. With double-headed express trains fighting their way through the rain storms high up on the Mendip Hills or the 18.05 Bath to Binegar train with its one solitary coach – it is all part of the mystique of the S&D. In this new book I have tried to bring back those days. I hope you all enjoy the new volume as much as I have enjoyed finding the new photographs and the people's memories of this marvellous railway.

A big hug goes to my wife and best friend Christine, who has kept an eye on my computer work and has been an absolute wizard on the digital scanner in repairing and cleaning old photographs for the new book. A special mention of thanks to Phil Collins for writing the foreword and to publisher Tim Graham who has again done a superb job in the design of the book and for putting up with me when I'm in pester mode.

I would like to express my very sincere thanks to Keith Barrett for the great amount of help and time he has given me with his first-hand knowledge and his photographs of the S&D. To Andy Moon who has again been of considerable help with my books from day one. To my good mate Roy Pitman who goes through the proof-reading in fine detail as do Keith Barrett, Christine Hammond, Irene Hammond, Gillies Watson, Frances Bristow, fellow railway author Richard Derry, Graham Hooper, Ian Matthews, Jim Milton, Allan Stanistreet and the late Cliff Smith.

I would like to acknowledge all the contributors of photographs and memories, without whom we would not have a book. Again Tim Deacon has come up with a list of S&D staff names which are so important in a book like this.

Many others have been of great help and assistance to me and I would like to record my sincere thanks to The Somerset & Dorset Railway Trust, *Western Gazette Press*, Shepton Mallet Model Railway Society, Dennis Ashill, Wally Moon, Bob Downes, Jason Baker, Richard Dagger, Ken Coffin, Ivor Willshire, George Tucker, Len West, Ian Matthews, John Stamp, Bruce Briant, John Simms, Dr. Peter Cattermole, Steve Bletso, Mona Pitman, Len Taylor, Dave Boston, Billy Conibeer, Brian

Winter, Maurice Cook, Ted Drew, Ivor Ridout, Mick Elliott, Vic Freak, Mary and Les Haines, Ron Hatcher, George Welch, Jim Jewell, Stan Morey, Gerald Box, David Strawbridge, Percy Parsons, Reg Biffin, Frank Staddon, Norman Ashman, Richard Barton, Kate and Stan Blacker, Joan and Alan Gregory, Ron Foxwell, Graham O'Donnell, Dennis Mitchell, Roger Raisey, Terry Kelly, Joy Church, Keran A. Waldon and Chris Osment.

As many photographs are from personal collections, a reader may well recognise a photograph that they may have taken. In this case I offer my apologies in advance for not being able to credit you.

If you are interested in keeping the memory of the S&D alive, three groups exist with these aims: The Somerset & Dorset Railway Trust at Washford; The Somerset & Dorset Railway Heritage Trust at Midsomer Norton; and The North Dorset Railway Trust at Shillingstone.

The S&D to me is about people who worked on the line and it is only fitting that we should remember those who have passed on since my last book. Our thoughts are with the families of Bill Butler, Reg Darke, Gordon Hatcher, Ern Hooker, Dick Isaacs, Arthur King, Rodney Scovell, Cliff Smith, Frank Staddon and Sid White.

Alan Hammond
Minehead, 2005

Unfortunately not Genesis but the well-known Essex group Quota Plus, which the author played for in the 1970s. The line up left to right are, Dave Buthlay (guitarist), Alan Hammond (guitarist), Dave Moore (singer), Brian Rowland (drummer) and Dave Hughes (organist). If only we could turn the clock back?

(*above*) Bath Green Park station for the Somerset & Dorset Joint Railway in 1954. The area directly behind the photographer was flattened by the Baedeker air raids of April 1942. It is remarkable that apart from the loss of glass from the overall roof, the station survived virtually unscathed. (*Norman Simmons/Hugh Davies collection*)

(*right*) Dave Boston worked on the S&D as a signalman. His first job on the railway was as a van guard boy. He is seen here in 1949 aged 17, with his bay mare Dolly, No.343, winning first prize for the cleanest harness and grooming in the horse contest. This event was held at the yearly horse show competition. (*Dave Boston collection*)

(*above*) A very early shot taken in 1928, of S&D 4-4-0 No.44 at Bath Green Park, about to take out a train to Bournemouth. Note the smoke coming out of the chimney, there must have been a fair amount of wind about. (*Jack Hobbs collection*)

(*right*) A Peak diesel stands at the same platform. To the left is the well-known railway photographer Norman Lockett with Arthur Rowett, who was a well-respected S&D railwayman for many years. (*Keran A. Waldon collection*)

(*left*) Nigel Pass looking very wet in his waterproofs, having his picture taken in front of 9F No.92214 (now preserved) at Bath Green Park in 1964. (*Brian Pass*)

(*below*) 53810 surrounded by the Ian Allan loco spotters club (Taunton branch) at Bath Green Park shed in 1959. Included in the group are Michael Henley, Brian Fisher, Barry Totterdell, Raymond Turner, Michael Pollard, Brian Singh, Andrew Wood and Roger Bond. (*Peter Triggs*)

Bath Green Park staff in the 1950s. The photograph is thought to include Peter Godfrey, Bert Mundy, Reg Glass, Bill Wise, Jack Hopkins, Dickie Weeks, Edgar Pothecary, Ted Hefferman, Sid Broad, Ivor Meader, Bill Wiltshire, Claude Hickland, Charlie Coles, Lew Adams, Polly Grymes, Dorothy Dolling, Joyce Ainsworth, Clement Bartholomew, Arthur Rowett, Ted Francis, Harry Wolley, A. Pleece, Jack Frapwell, Mr. Cooper, Allan Wilson, Jack Wotley, Jack Hookey, Mr. Stowe, J. Wake, Bill Wilds, Fred Toller and W. Stagg. (*Keran A. Waldon collection*)

(*left*) Arthur King (senior) enjoying his retirement party at the Newbridge public house in the 1960s, after many years as a driver on the S&D. This inn was the nearest to Bath Green Park where Arthur worked. Note the King special, I wonder what loco this was modelled on? (*Jim Jewell collection*)

(*right*) Railwayman Wally Moon's son Richard, aged 11, is standing proudly between S&D drivers Cecil Waldron (left) and Norman Gibbons on the day 9F *Evening Star* arrived at Bath loco, c.1962. (*Wally Moon*)

A lovely picture, but a sad event at Bath Green Park, as guard Percy Hamblin says goodbye to driver Cecil Waldron (nicknamed Smokebox). Fireman Wayne Mayo is looking out of the cab of BR class 4 No. 80043. The date was 5 March 1966, the last day of normal service on the S&D. (*John Stamp*)

(*above*) Bath Green Park Motive Power Depot on 5 March 1966. A line of superfluous locomotives awaits its final journey to the scrapyard. I wonder if any of these engines escaped the torch. (*Wayne Mayo collection*)

(*below*) An earlier shot of the depot. From left to right: 2P No.40563, Standard class 4 No.75073 and 7F No.53800. On the extreme right is the coach body used for mutual improvement classes. The positioning of the locomotives is reminiscent of Rev. Awdry's *Thomas the Tank Engine* stories. (*Dennis Mitchell*)

(*right*) The down Cleethorpes leaves Bath Green Park behind a class 4F and 7F No.53807. Looking ahead is driver Derek Howcutt from Templecombe shed. (*R.K. Blencowe collection*)

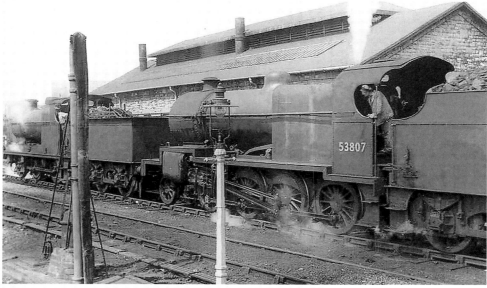

(*left*) Lady cleaners at Bath Green Park in front of 4-4-0 No.71, c.1900s. These ladies carried out a first-class job and were an important part of the railway. (*Desmond Tidball collection*)

London and South Western Ry.

787

From WATERLOO

TO

BATH

Via Templecombe.

(*right*) Railway enthusiast Geoff Bannister stands on the buffer beam of 7F No.53809 at Bath shed in 1959. (*Geoff Bannister collection*)

Fireman Wayne Mayo tightens up the smokebox door of Bath Green Park engine BR class 5 No.73001. Driver Bert Read is by the side of the motion. (*Wayne Mayo collection*)

What a great shot of 8F No.48309 engulfed in smoke and steam, hauling a dead engine up the steep incline from the S&D shed at Bath Green Park to the goods shed on 3 February 1965. (*Paul Strong*)

(*above*) An atmospheric shot of the last service train into Bath Green Park station with Standard class 4 No.80041 piloting No.80043 which is engulfed in steam. (*Wayne Mayo collection*)

(*below*) 2P No.40634 pilots 9F No.92006 with the up Pines Express into Bath Green Park on 31 July 1961. (*John Cornelius*)

(*above*) S&D driver and later foreman Len West, is seen here in front of 9F No. 92220 *Evening Star* at Bath Green Park. Len worked on the railway for over 50 years. How many of us will work for one company for that amount of time? (*Len West collection*)

(*below*) Superpower for a short train working, of two ex-S&D locos. Fowler 7F No.53807 together with 4F No.44558, head a train of ex-LMS coaches with a SR utility van past Bellotts Road on a very wet day in June 1964. (*R.J. Coles*)

(*left*) Mates together on the footplate of BR class 5 No.73051, are George Welch (left) and Charlie Watkins. (*George Welch collection*)

(*below*) A reminder of past glories as Stanier LMS class 5 No.44963 coasts in to Midford with a down train. (*Roger Raisey*)

(*above*) A party of interested onlookers in 1949, as 2P No.509 pilots an LMS Black 5 with a train from the south on to the single line section passing Midford station. It is interesting that British Railways was now 18 months old, but the 2P is still carrying its LMS number. The leading car in Twinhoe Lane looks interesting as well. (*Millbrook House Ltd/R.S. Carpenter collection*)

(*below*) 7F No.53802, with a goods train heading south, is testing the tablet catcher apparatus under supervision at Midford in 1950. (*R.K. Blencowe collection*)

(*above*) 34006 *Bude* and 34057 *Biggin Hill* passing Wellow en-route for Bath Green Park with an LCGB Rail Tour on 5 March 1966. (*R.J. Coles*)

(*above*) 4F No.44424 in harness with West Country No.34041 *Wilton*, as it threads its way past Shoscombe and Single Hill Halt with the down Pines Express in 1959. (*Keith Barrett collection*)

(*below*) Two ladies wait on the platform as BR class 4 No.75071 coasts into Shoscombe and Single Hill Halt with a local passenger train. (*Roger Holmes/Hugh Davies collection*)

(*above*) A superb view of a pair of 4Fs, Nos. 44045 and 44424 rounding the curve near Radstock in 1959. (*Keith Barrett collection*)

(*below*) A pre-war scene as 7F No.13801 races towards Radstock with a down freight in 1937. (*Keith Barrett collection*)

Wally Moon

Wartime service in the Royal Navy took me completely around the world as a wireless telegraphist, ending in the busy flying control at Lee-on-Solent before returning to Civvie Street. At the ripe old age of 21 my immediate objectives were to obtain a permanent job and marry my fiancée. Visiting the local employment office I was asked if I would like to be an engine driver. My response was that I had never once considered the job but as it was permanent I was interested. 'Go round to the S&D engine shed' said Mr. Alex Hann, the manager; 'Tell Charlie Baker, the chargehand fitter, that I sent you'. Two days later I was interviewed in the Bath LMS loco department main office by chief clerk, Bill Hack; the Dickensian office lacked only quill pens.

Mr. Hack's first remarks were to inform me that I would not get my gold watch on retirement at 65, because my total service could only be 43 years and 10 months. 45-year retirement gold watches had just been introduced. Medical and preliminaries completed, I started work at Radstock locomotive depot in November 1946. One month later I was fireman to driver Aubrey Pearce, a man with a good brain and a born instructor on the locomotive. He was also an excellent first-aider to the injured. During wartime Aubrey trained over 1,000 people in First Aid and was twice honoured by the St. John Ambulance Association to which the Railway Ambulance Service was linked.

Like the Royal Navy it was a man's world except for Catherine Parker (later Berryman), a wartime signal-woman who remained for

Catherine Parker worked on the S&D in the 1940s and 50s in Radstock East signalbox where this photo was taken and in Writhlington box for nine years. Other people who worked there included Doris Dorley, Ted Morris, Walt Woods, Bert Haines and Les Willsher. Catherine said to me she couldn't drive a car but could drive a steam loco, having had plenty of tuition from the lads at Radstock shed. (*Catherine Berryman, née Parker, collection*)

many more years in Radstock East signalbox which controlled access to and from the main line – a fine lady and very good at her job.

The drivers were unique individuals who had great pride in their work, all had started at the age of 14 and were expected to work until they were 65. The LMS had no pension scheme, a letter of thanks was all they got. My starting wage was £4.10s.0d per week for the first month, then £5 afterwards. My first day was on the little 0-4-0 Lancs & Yorks yard shunter (nicknamed Pug up North but called the Jocker at Radstock). Work involved visiting Middle Pit, Radstock Gas Works and the old colliery sidings at Clandown which were opposite the old quarry cottages. One siding was full of empty wooden wagons with MTD boldly painted in white on each side. I learnt that this meant Ministry of Transport Derequisite, in other words unfit for further use. I expressed surprise that the planks had not been removed for firewood. Aubrey suggested I climbed up and looked inside the wagons, which I did and found all the floor boards missing.

The track in the sidings was privately owned and of lightweight construction. The sleepers and rails had sunk below ground in many places and one pair of wheels continually ran off the track, then came back on again. Later I found many sidings full of MTD wagons. In effect most of these were worn out or patched up.

The Radstock home signal was very high, in fact higher than the church tower. I remember John Webb climbing up the signal on one occasion carrying two heavy lamps

(*left*) Passing through Radstock with only a brakevan is 7F No.53807 on its return journey to Bath. On the right can be seen the abutment of bridge No.37 Marble Arch which carried sidings to Tyning Colliery. (*Roger Raisey*)

(*below*) Two Radstock engines with Frank Kemp on the footplate of the Saddle Tank No.11202 shunting Sentinel No.7190. (*Wally Moon collection*)

on a cold and rainy day, using only one hand to grip the iron ladder rungs. It was really a job for a steeplejack. Nowadays there would be a dozen Health and Safety regulations to overcome before ascending.

The S&D over the Mendips was built on the side of land which was difficult to maintain due to water draining from higher ground. Between Radstock and Midsomer Norton ballast was replaced beneath the track regularly and a 15mph speed restriction remained permanently in force.

Footplatemen had a real sense of humour, if someone arrived at Bath shed rest room boasting about their performance with a particular train, the round clock was soon taken off the wall and presented to them.

I recall my first visit to Bournemouth Pavilion when inspector Charlie Brown from Derby gave a lecture to all Mutual Improvement classes on the former LMS (MICs were voluntarily attended classes where drivers passed on their knowledge of the locomotives, plus rules and regulations to the younger firemen). In his opening remarks he said a certain footplate inspector was retiring and he felt it would be nice if best wishes were sent to him from the conference. There was the longest silence ever, at least 1½ minutes, then a burly driver with a Midlands accent stood up and said: 'If the inspector really is retiring and there is no hope of him ever coming back again I propose that best wishes should be sent from the conference'. The pavilion erupted with applause and laughter.

Like the drivers, every locomotive had its own personality. Some would steam on a lighted match and others made you depressed by just looking at the number on the smokebox. I once suggested to Mr. Harold Morris, shedmaster at Bath, and a man well respected and worthy of the title, that he tried an experiment by changing over engine numbers to see if there was any improvement.

I recall one of my early morning trips with driver Bert Ashleigh. We banked the 03.30 goods up from Radstock to Masbury Summit, after whistling loud and long as we started together. Cottages in Waterloo Road, Radstock were only yards from the main line and the noise must have been alarming. It was very foggy and Bert seemed to be looking over the side all the way up to the top of the Mendips. Returning (still foggy) Bert stopped four times and picked up four rabbits which had been struck by the up mail train, stopping each time within two yards of the rabbit. When Bert retired we gave him a clock and a farewell party, something

unheard of by the older drivers. I visited Lanes the jeweller and clockmaker's shop in Radstock with insufficient money to purchase the clock I really liked. He let me have some money off when I mentioned Bert's retirement. Pushing my luck I asked if he could engrave a little plate and attach it to the front; he agreed with a smile. Bert handed me his engineman's metal box on his last day; I still treasure it.

My first trip on the class 7F engine was in February 1947, a very severe winter. I was married on 1 February and my wife's bouquet was frozen in the vase in the bedroom. The tulips and stems were still frozen one month later. On this first trip we travelled wrong road from Masbury to Shepton Mallet. Binegar stationmaster Norman Down accompanied us as the official pilot. Passing over the high Bath Road Viaduct at Shepton Mallet I looked over the left-hand side of the engine when suddenly I was looking through the sleepers to the highway below. I shouted to the driver that the adjoining track had gone. The pilot and driver were discussing the merits of Welton Rovers football team's performance the previous Saturday. Obviously they anticipated my reaction and tried not to smile. Looking over the driver's side I could see all the platelayers resting against the viaduct parapet wall and appearing unconcerned. It was some time later that I realized the two tracks, 60 feet in the air were supported on separate bridge arches when the line was doubled.

Radstock crews worked full loads of mineral, coal from Norton Hill Colliery and stone from Emborough Quarry, with a bank engine in the rear. On the return trip we worked tender-first, pulling 40 empty 16-ton wagons the seven miles from Evercreech to Masbury Summit and then all downhill to Midsomer Norton. When the north east winds blew it was not only very cold and sometimes wet but the wind in the empty wagons almost doubled the weight. Nowhere in the country was more skill and effort needed. Driver Aubrey Pearce spontaneously broke into song (la-la-la-la) every time we passed over the summit. Improved lubrication to the cylinders would have improved these class 7 engines, which constantly emitted clouds of leaking steam.

Aubrey Pearce's brother Maurice (later a driver at Saltley, Birmingham) was the fireman on class 7 engine No.13809 (then No.89) when it crashed in Bath after the driver and fireman were overcome by fumes in Combe Down Tunnel on 20 November 1929. Driver Henry Jennings was killed, also inspector John Norman in Bath yard and railway clerk Jack Loader (taking a short cut home) was struck by flying debris. The fireman and guard Christopher Wagner survived. Every time we stepped on this engine, now numbered 53809 Aubrey would say '20th November 1929'.

I was fireman to Horace Clark when the signalman at Evercreech Junction north box opened the window to shout out 'It's a boy'. Horace could not believe that I would come to work and leave my wife at home. I calmed his nerves by informing him that my mother-in-law was in attendance and the district nurse lived nearby. I never lost a day through sickness or any other reason but I admit to being late a few times.

On Saturdays during the summer workings and at other times when spare, our services were required at Bath. As firemen we looked forward to express passenger experience with Bath drivers. Going north we usually worked as far as Cheltenham before changing over for the return trip and going south to Bournemouth West or assisting by double heading over the Mendips to Evercreech Junction, returning with another train.

I recall three journeys with Bath drivers, firstly a mid-week trip with driver Danny Alexander with the Pines Express from Bath to Gloucester. We were informed that the return Pines was running late with steaming problems and a replacement engine was being made ready at Gloucester loco depot. On arrival, both the driver and fireman looked shattered. At that moment someone arrived to inform Danny that the relief engine was derailed when leaving the shed. I examined the fire and found clinker right up to the firehole door with 140lbs steam instead of 250lbs and less than half a glass of water. Driver Alexander did not complain, swear or stamp his feet: 'We'll pull up to Tuffley to clear the station platform and then assess the situation', he said. He needed to open the large ejector instead of the small one to release the vacuum brake. Working hard, we arrived at Tuffley, no better, no worse. There was a 2½ mile speed restriction ahead due to relaying operations and we eventually crawled home to Bath. Arriving at Bath Green Park station, Harold Morris, the shedmaster and another official both shook hands and thanked Danny for getting the train to Bath for its onward journey to Bournemouth. Moving to the front of our engine, to remove one of the headlamps to the rear before proceeding to shed, I noticed the whole underside of the smokebox was red hot and the smokebox drawing in air. This was obviously the beginning of the problem. Arriving on the drop pit I took a spanner, brush and shovel to examine the smokebox. A driver nearby said in a Somerset twang: 'Casn't thou not read that smokebox has SC written on it, that's a self cleaner'. I ignored his remarks and finally opened the door. Red hot ash was nearly up to the top of the blast pipe, covering the lower tubes; it came out like a volcano erupting, causing me to jump from the footplate and the observant driver to scamper to safety. Had we stopped in Wickwar Tunnel, Danny and I would have been roasted alive.

On another trip I was fireman to driver Arthur Selman with an Armstrong Whitworth 0-6-0 tender engine on the 09.00 Sunshine Express, Bath to Bournemouth West. These engines were known for rough riding due to having no bogie wheels. The driver stood on a wooden box type platform raising him about 10 inches to improve visibility of the road ahead. On arrival at Bournemouth our guard Ted Francis informed us that we could not turn the engine on Branksome Triangle because the crane was stabled there for use the next day. We also learned that the turntable in Bournemouth Central's Southern depot was not performing well and a string of engines were queuing to turn. Arthur suggested working tender-first back to Evercreech Junction and turning there before continuing to Bath. 'Otherwise', he said, 'we'll not have time for a meal.' In the circumstances I agreed, knowing we had a good steaming engine and a canvas sheet to protect us against the elements and dust. All went well until we reached Cole curve north of Wincanton, which carried a permanent speed restriction. As the engine lurched through the curve Arthur put all his weight on the brass injector steam valve control wheel to steady himself. Unbelievably the wheel came away from the valve spindle and Arthur standing on the elevated box went hurtling backwards through the gap between engine and tender. Doing a full-length dive I grabbed his lone foot pressing it against the handrail. After a marathon effort by the two of us Arthur was back on board. We were both exhausted and looking out of the fireman's side of the engine I could see we were approaching Bruton Road Crossing. Arthur resumed control and slowed the engine into a stop at Evercreech Junction after cursing all the worn-out engines, all the fitters and their ancestors. Just another day.

Fortunately guard Ted Francis knew nothing of the incident. Arthur who was known for his forthright manner must have said thanks very quietly. On arrival home my wife remarked: 'I should think you had been rolling around in wet coal by the appearance of your overalls, which were clean on this morning'. How very true. I don't expect Arthur drove any more express trains tender-first. He must have been bruised for several weeks.

Another Saturday return trip involved a stopping train from Bath to Templecombe with driver Vic Hunt. We followed the last of the up holiday specials, approaching Moorwood immediately before the Emborough Quarry up sidings, when three detonators exploded. Vic stopped the train promptly. The ganger Cliff Lovell had found the track buckled in the afternoon heat at the point where the Quarry siding joins the main line, and ran to stop us in time. Cliff was gasping and asked for a drink. I gave him the dregs from my tea can which he said was lovely.

Moorwood signalbox was closed and the guard protected the train in the rear as he walked back to Binegar signalbox to report the situation. Norman Down, stationmaster at Binegar, was normally on call on summer Saturdays but on holiday at this time. The on-call relief man had to come from Bath and after 1 hour 40 minutes he arrived on the down road, riding on the Radstock motorized trolley driven by Walt Weeks. As he stopped on the way to Binegar his remarks were classical: 'I'm going to Binegar to set up single line working, so when authorized, hurry back to Binegar as we don't want any delay'. In the meantime inspector Bob Hardiman of the permanent way department had arrived by car from Shepton Mallet and, together with Cliff Lovell, pulled the track back into line and gave the all clear. We proceeded after more than two hours. It caused great excitement amongst the passengers, all looking out of the windows and chatting to each other.

Fred Pearce, who was a shunter and guard at Radstock, told me about the first day he started as a junior porter at Midsomer Norton station. He was instructed to light the fires in the waiting room and the stationmaster's office. Fred did so but when the stationmaster arrived he complained that his office was smoky. Fred was ordered to remove the fire then take the hatchet and go into the wood adjacent to the up line and cut a holly bush branch. The stationmaster said: 'I'll show you how to clean a chimney. It will be something you will never forget.' A rope was secured to the V of the branch and the other end secured to a weight which was taken up a ladder and dropped down the chimney. The stem of the holly bush was inserted in the chimney and the stationmaster and other staff started to pull. Part

way down the bush became stuck so firmly that the builders had to dismantle the whole chimney stack to free it. 'I shall never forget it', said Fred. 'That's what the stationmaster said to me and I never shall.'

In my eleventh year of service I was passed as a driver by chief inspector Willoughby of Eastleigh. I reached my top driving rate of pay after completing 864 driving turns (288 x 3 years).

A sad event I recall, was when driver Charlie Rawlings was at the end of a First Aid practice night and he was expecting his son Tom to collect him from the hall in his car. A police officer arrived to tell him Tom had been killed in a road accident. On another sad occasion driver Horace Clark received news that his son Eric had been badly wounded just before V.E. day. Eric lost an eye and an arm. Horace was heartbroken, when everybody else was celebrating.

We once had a relief guard from the Southern Region on a coal train. At the end of the journey he gave driver Aubrey Pearce a green lost time ticket. We had lost two minutes in one section and made up two minutes in another. The form was as impressive as a test match score card. Aubrey congratulated him on his neat and precise presentation whilst screwing it up and throwing it in the firebox. 'We don't use them forms on the Darset'. he remarked. The poor guard stood open mouthed in amazement.

Before the big freeze and heavy snow of 1963 a large flock of chattering geese passed overhead flying south. Telegraph lineman, Fred Mitchell was present and asked me where the flies went in the winter time. It was very cold and I replied: 'Not to Binegar'. Fred showed me an insulator he had replaced; inside it was packed with flies. The railway telephone system was powered by simple battery cells stored beneath the signalboxes, which provided enough warmth to keep the packed flies alive. Fred was a nice fellow, he was captain of the first ambulance team I competed with. In time I took over from Aubrey Pearce as captain of Radstock No. 1 team. The same team also belonged to the voluntary British Red Cross Society. We reached the all-Britain finals in London. Out of eight regional teams we came 2nd in 1951 and 3rd in 1952. Other railway first-aiders were Laurie Anstice, Eric Wilson, Fred Griffin, Joe Crouchen, Charlie Rawlings, Herbert Packer, Bill Coombes, Jack Tapper, Walt Woods, Bob Ryan, Jesse Williams, Jock Summerville, Joe Bowsher and Ken Evans. Police, firemen and coal miners all joined us for weekly practices.

(*left*) Radstock Railway Ambulance class on the occasion of driver Charlie Rawlings' retirement.
Back row, left to right: Joe Crouchen, Laurie Anstice, Eric Wilson, Wally Moon, Joe Bowsher and Jesse Williams.
Front row, left to right: Jack Tapper, Aubrey Pearce, Charlie Rawlings, Bill Coombes and Bob Ryan.
(*Wally Moon collection*)

(*below*) Shield winners in 1956 at the Bristol District First Aid competition are Radstock railwaymen. Left to right, Mr. Goodfellow presenting the shield, Joe Bowsher, Bill Coombes, Joe Crouchen, Wally Moon (captain) and Eric Wilson. (*Wally Moon collection*)

On one occasion a member of the permanent way staff was injured and I sent his colleague to collect a first-aid box. Returning with the shiny black and white box I found it contained a piece of roller bandage about 15 inches long and nearly black, and an accident report book. In my own haversack I carried a large wound dressing which I kept for emergencies so I was able to use this. Quietly I made it known that this could have been very embarrassing if there was a serious accident. At a later competition an official informed me that I had cost the region thousands of pounds as they re-stocked all first-aid boxes. It was a good-humoured comment.

On 4 March 1966 I was the driver of the last steam engine in use at Radstock which was a Bagnall side Tank No. 47276; it was taken to Bath for a sad onward journey to the engines' graveyard in South Wales. As I said goodbye to the S&D my thoughts were to the workmates I knew, like Bert Ash, Ray Fish, Bert Haines, Phil Crouchen, Charlie Burge, Alan Dowling, Bill Kelly, Ken Shearn, David Jones, Jack Wescombe,

Jimmy Angell, Dennis Curtis, Dennis Love, David Humphries, Tom Newman, Desmond Kemp, Bert Webster, Tony Young and Dennis Jones. Not one person was interested in saying farewell to steam although the historical event had been given national publicity. That weekend the S&D was linked by a spur to the Great Western line just south of the level crossing so that Writhlington colliery coal could be sent to the power station via Bristol and a diesel shunter was brought in for use by drivers Aubrey Pearce and Frank Kemp who had been for diesel training.

With the end of steam I left. Harold Morris came to Radstock and gave me two books which originally belonged to Alfred Whitaker, S&D Locomotive Superintendent. It was very sad; as I said goodbye to Mr. Morris and Charlie Baker, I had a lump in my throat and felt quite tearful. Later I joined the Somerset Ambulance Service and my voluntary interest became full-time. The rest, as they say, is history. I am now 79 years old supported by a wonderful family, four generations in total.

On the footplate at Radstock are Desmond Kemp (known as Jack) and Frank Kemp. (*Frank Kemp collection*)

(*left*) A Jinty Tank hauls a train of loaded coal wagons out of Norton Hill Colliery sidings and on to the main line at Midsomer Norton station. (*Frank Kemp collection*)

London and South Western Ry.
767
FROM WATERLOO TO
MIDSOMER NORTON

(*below*) A busy scene, as Standard class 4 No.75073 approaches Midsomer Norton station with a southbound Bournemouth train, passing Jinty No.47316 at Norton Hill siding in 1960. (*R.E. Toop*)

A photographer's delight at Midsomer Norton on a fine spring day in April 1957, as 2P No.40569 pilots BR Standard class 5 No.73047 with the southbound Pines Express. (*R.E. Toop*)

Down express passing Midsomer Norton station heading south, hauled by 2P No.40696 piloting West Country class No.34041 *Wilton*. The two leading coaches are still in early BR livery of crimson lake and cream, c.1957. (*J.W.T. House/C.L. Caddy collection*)

(*left*) The quality of this photograph taken at Midsomer Norton station in 1933 is not ideal. But with the size of the prize-winning cactus held by porter Fred Pearce next to signalman Fred Griffin, it is a must for the book. (*Somerset & Dorset Railway Heritage Trust collection*)

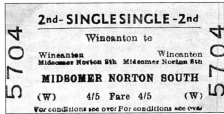

(*below*) Frank Packer and Joe Crouchen outside the Midsomer Norton goods shed in the 1920s. Note the milk churns on the horse-drawn dray. (*Mrs. M. Packer collection*)

(*above*) Driver Frank Kemp on the engine and fireman Wally Moon, topping up the side tanks at Chilcompton on 3F No.47308 between banking duties. Note Sheppard's sawmills on the right-hand side. This was a very cold spot when the north wind blew in the winter. (*Wally Moon collection*)

(*below*) Driver George Welch looks out of the cab of 7F No.53804 at Chilcompton in 1958. (*George Welch collection*)

(*above*) Two of the porters at Chilcompton station found time for humour with the stationmaster. On the horse are two of Fry's, Stratton-on-the-Fosse taxi/telegram employees purporting to be the Chilcompton and Stratton mounted battery brigade. (*David Strawbridge collection*)

(*below*) One of the old Sentinel lorries which were garaged at Broadway, Chilcompton, pictured around 1930 with drivers Charlie Charles and Ern Knowles. Charlie later died after an accident involving one of these steam lorries. These vehicles were much in demand taking coal to Chilcompton station. (*David Strawbridge collection*)

(*right*) Railway maintenance gang and dog in 1935 at the Chilcompton end of Iletts Tunnel. Left to right are Harry Walters, Frank Coles, Bill Southway, Bill Prior, Jack Foxwell, Dick Symes and Sam Tucker. (*Ron Foxwell collection*)

(*below*) Chilcompton and Radstock relaying gangs join forces for this group photo. Some of the names in the picture are Dick Symes, Jack Foxwell, Cliff Lovell, Frank Coles and Bill Prior. (*David Strawbridge collection*)

David Strawbridge

My earliest memory of the Somerset & Dorset Railway is when I lived at Wells Road, Chilcompton. I was five years old and with my friends ran the 200 metres or so across a meadow to the railway line near Fry's Well. Little did we know that the Great Western Turnpike Road had crossed this meadow 100 years before. Until 1836 this was the main coach and mail route from London to Cornwall. On climbing the embankment we had to avoid the carefully tended garden allotments bordering the line. In the 1930s, rail traffic was busy and we didn't have long to wait for a train. They were always an interest to us kids and the drivers would usually wave, although they were busy if coming up from Ilett's Tunnel because this section was one of the steepest in England. From the age of 7 to 17 I lived on the other side of the line in lower Chilcompton and when I was older and braver, I would foolishly stand in a shallow recess inside the long tunnel while a train rushed past, less than one metre away. For six of those ten years there was a war on and traffic was even busier with heavy loads of troops and armour. One such train consisted of eleven LMS corridor coaches, a restaurant car, a bogie van and 4 four-wheeled vans. There were two locomotives in front and one behind hauling a total of 17 vehicles. I once saw a train with an engine in the middle.

Following the bombing of Bath in 1942 many people came out on the evening trains from the city to sleep rough anywhere they could for safety. A favourite place was in the mill at Midsomer Norton. Seventy years before, the railway builders had spent their nights in a large empty mansion in Chilcompton called Norton Hall which stood conveniently near the line.

Other memories are of watching carts and lorries tipping their loads of coal from the village colliery into trucks at Chilcompton station. I also used to have my hair cut by signalman Bill Coombes in the exposed signalbox.

From near the station a footpath led to Bakers Lane and, because it was railway property, every Good Friday (no trains) the footpath was roped-off with a man guarding each end so that it could not become a right-of-way.

During the early part of the war a defence line was built alongside the railway. It was made up of a line of large blocks of concrete, five foot square and four feet apart stretching for perhaps 200 metres. There were pillboxes which had thick flat roofs with side slits from which the occupants could fire. There was a further 200 metres of wide deep trench before the next pillbox and another line of concrete blocks. These pillboxes were well camouflaged and some were made to look like hayricks; many of these still remain.

I travelled on the train from Chilcompton to Bath to attend Bath Technical College from 1944 to 1946. I cycled to the station to catch the 08.05 train and returned about 17.00. The trains were remarkably punctual considering there was a war on. Our village station was crowded with adults and students, travelling mostly to Midsomer Norton and Bath. Our station was the nearest to Downside R.C. School which had 500 resident students which meant many packed trains at the beginning and the end of each term. The stationmaster Stan Ashley would recruit extra staff to help the three porters, Walt Kerton, Sid Smith and Laurie Dando to cope with all the luggage. A little later Frank Germaine was added to the team. Some other members of staff who worked at Chilcompton included Frank Staddon, Cliff Brown, Percy Hamblin, William Jackson, Stan Routley, Ron Pearce, John Webb, Tom Tamblyn, Michael Reakes, Victor Burge and William Stacey.

One sobering memory for me was one morning on the way to college when we were approaching Shoscombe and Single Hill Halt. A stone came from nowhere and hit my best friend Roy Atkins, who was looking out of the window, causing him to lose one of his eyes.

One might think that our daily journeys to Bath by rail in those days might have been monotonous but they were anything but that. Today we travel to Bath by bus or car and can see very little except hedges and buildings from our restricted seats, but by train on the old S&D it was always a delight. For instance only a minute after leaving the station we would have a panoramic view of old Chilcompton from our spectacular position high on the hillside. Then views of Midsomer Norton, before levelling at Radstock where the gate across the main road would always be open. One mile on and with Writhlington Colliery behind us we would be weaving our way through the hills and meadows of Shoscombe, Wellow and Midford, which made as picturesque a ride as one could wish for. Then the contrast of the two tunnels under Combe Down and we would be practically in the middle of Bath, a little over 40 minutes after setting out. We would arrive at busy Bath Green Park station and within minutes would be outside with scarcely a backward glance at the excellent neo-Georgian façade which graced the main entrance. What an irretrievable loss it was to those railway communities when the line was closed under the Beeching axe in the interests of progress.

In the 1960s when our four children were small, my wife and I would often take them up to the Bakers Lane Bridge where they could lean over the parapet and would be covered in lovely white smoke and wave to the friendly footplate crew, which included Wally Moon, Eric Wilson, John Stamp, John Sawyer, Howard Reynolds, Ron Bean, Eric Webber and Mike Ryall. The Bakers Lane Bridge still has several dates of 1874 inscribed on the roof.

On the last day of the S&D my wife drove me and our four children to Shepton Mallet station where once Max Shore, Emily Poole, Len and Rose Brooks used to work, to catch the last daylight train to Chilcompton. She then drove back to Chilcompton to meet us. This was the first and last time our young children travelled on the S&D and it was an experience they still remember much to the envy of their friends.

The extremely smart and well-liked Chilcompton station-master Stan Routley, stands on the platform in the 1950s. (*Joan & Alan Gregory collection*)

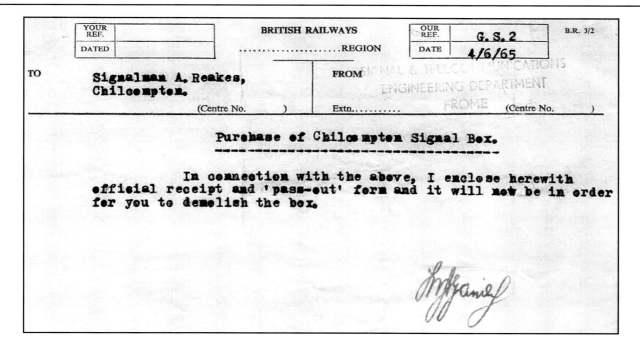

Memories of glorious days of steam as 2P No.40563 stops at Chilcompton with a local passenger train. Everything at the station looks neat and tidy. (*R.K. Blencowe collection*)

(*above*) Permanent way men at Binegar station. From left to right: John Earl, Henry Kitley, Cliff Lovell, unknown. (*Robert Kitley collection*)

(*below*) Behind the simmering 3F is Binegar station house, where stationmaster Norman Down once lived with his wife Dorothy. In the front of the picture are permanent way men Jack Foxwell (left) and Bill Prior, c.1935. (*Ron Foxwell collection*)

(*above*) Caricature of Michael Reakes, the signalman at Binegar and Chilcompton, drawn by the Evercreech New stationmaster Reg Jeans. (*Tessa Eyers collection*)

(*below*) From left to right: Frank Coles, Harry Walters, Dick Symes, Bill Prior and Jack Foxwell on the track at Binegar. I wonder what the railway dog was called? (*Ron Foxwell collection*)

(*above*) LMS 4-4-0 No.628 ambles into Binegar with an up local heading for Bath Green Park, c.1937. (*Keith Barrett collection*)

(*below*) 7F No.53809 hauling a number of wagons through Binegar in the 1950s. Underneath the veranda a very clean motor bike is at the ready for the signalman when he finishes his shift. (*Keith Barrett collection*)

(*left*) On a bitterly cold day with snow on the ground, Binegar station looks ghostly and desolate with nobody around. Full marks to the photographer for turning out in terrible weather to take this splendid photo.
(*Stations.UK collection*)

(*below*) Summer with steam in 1964, as 4F No.44422 comes out of the shadow of Winsor Hill Tunnel with a local train. (*David Walden*)

Breasting the summit at Masbury are 3F 0-6-0T No.47316 and 7F No.53806. How neat the ballast looks. (*E.W. Fry/R.K. Blencowe collection*)

A superb portrait of BR Standard No.80081 as it approaches Shepton Mallet Charlton Road station with the 13.10 Bath Green Park to Templecombe train in 1965. (*Paul Strong*)

(*above*) An elevated view from the footbridge at Shepton Mallet, of 2P No.40563 and an unidentified Standard with a passenger train for Bath. (*Norman Simmons/Hugh Davies collection*)

(*below*) Standard class 4 No.75007, introduced in 1951 with a weight of 69 tons, is seen here at Shepton Mallet with a local from Bath. Note the motor trolley housed on the left of the picture. (*Keith Barrett collection*)

(*above*) Driver Lou Long (left) and fireman Rodney Scovell enjoy having their photo taken on the footplate. (*SDRT collection*)

(*below*) BR Standard 4 No.76014 shows her worth, as it passes Evercreech New with an up express. It must be a cold day as the station buildings and the signalbox all have their fires burning. (*David Lawrence/Hugh Davies collection*)

The remains of Evercreech Junction North signalbox, taken high up from a signal. It was mysteriously burned out after the last train had passed on the final Saturday evening on 5 March 1966. It stands silent and gaunt, but defiant as ever, symbolizing the valiant efforts of those who tried to keep the line open. (*David Walden*)

This classic shot at Evercreech Junction shows 41242 taking on water. The fireman Ray Coates is perched on the boiler as driver Fritz Lawrence manoeuvres the wheel. (*Roger Holmes/Hugh Davies collection*)

Another thirsty engine at Evercreech is ex-LMS class 3 No.40098 with Mike Fudge on the platform and George Eason on top of the engine, c.1961. (*R.K. Blencowe collection*)

(*left*) Three railway characters at the Junction. From left to right: shunter Charlie Vaughan, guard Jimmy Yelling and foreman Vic Freak. (*Zoe Stowe collection*)

(*below*) Two porters enjoy having their photo taken on a summer's day at Evercreech. From left to right: Albert Taylor and David Kerle. (*Vic Freak collection*)

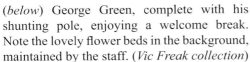

(*below*) George Green, complete with his shunting pole, enjoying a welcome break. Note the lovely flower beds in the background, maintained by the staff. (*Vic Freak collection*)

(*below*) A caricature of an S&D railwayman enjoying a pint at *The Railway Hotel* in Evercreech, drawn by stationmaster Reg Jeans. (*Shepton & District Railway Society collection*)

(*above*) *The Railway Hotel*, Evercreech Junction darts team of 1959/60. From left to right, back row: Reg Butt, Reg George, Ken Atkins (shunter), Bill Pippen (porter), Ernie Riggs, Fred Thick (signalman) and Derek ('Tanker') Jones (driver); front row Fred Box (crossing keeper), Cyril Richards, Mary Jewell (landlady) and Henry Cox. (*Mary Haines, née Jewell collection*)

(*below*) Guard Ted Christopher (left) and porter Gerald Box pose at Evercreech Junction. (*Mrs. M. Brown collection*)

Hard at work in 1949 is 0-6-0 Johnson 3F No.3204 with a rake of wagons on an up freight at Evercreech Junction. The crew member posing for the photo is Harry Jeans. (*R.K. Blencowe collection*)

A schoolboy's dream in the cab of 3F No.43218 at Evercreech Junction, with such an array of S&D personalities. In the cab are Vic Freak (left), schoolboy Richard Barton and Les Haines. On the track bed is Malcolm Hatherall (left) and the one and only Ronald (Chummy) Andrews, c.1955. (*Richard Barton collection*)

Evercreech Junction sets the scene for an acrobatic George Eason, as he climbs on top of 2-6-2T No.40098, c.1961. It looks a windy day at the Junction. (*R.K. Blencowe collection*)

Gerald Box

Bruton Road Crossing, Lamyatt, Shepton Mallet, Somerset, an address written by the Box family for many years. It is now only a memory and a ghost for many a traveller who goes past the old S&D crossing. Long gone are the days when West Countrys, 2Ps, Bulldogs, Fowler 4Fs, Midland Black 5s, and the old 7Fs went past the crossing, some at great speeds which rattled the window panes and sprayed smoke and smuts over the house. Lengthman Alf Russell used to walk the line from Evercreech Junction to Cole on a regular basis. With a key hammer in his hand, he knocked in the wooden keys that held the rails to the chairs that had loosened or dropped out from the vibrations of the trains belting by. When a train went by the crossing at speed, I would sometimes stand by the fence and look at the track bouncing up and down with the weight, and water would splash out from under the sleepers.

A photo taken from Evercreech Junction signalbox of ganger Alf Russell with his trusty key hammer. (*Vic Freak collection*)

About 08.30 each morning the school train would pass by with pupils going to Cole station, to go to either Sunny Hill Girls School or to Sexey's Boys School, both on the outskirts of Bruton. The train was usually pulled by a 2P or a Black 5. One morning looking out of the window whilst having breakfast, my dad shouted out, 'Look what's coming'. To my utter surprise it was being pulled by a Southern T9, the only one I had ever seen in my life, it looked like a greyhound. During the night previously the rostered engine from Templecombe to Bath had a hot box and the only available engine at hand was the T9.

A sad memory I recall was when relief crossing keeper Joe Kemp died. He often worked the crossing when mum and dad, or Roy Osborne, were on holiday. During the 1962/3 bad winter, Joe was found frozen to death on the track in the snow between Evercreech New and Elbow Corner Crossing. November 5th was a good day on the crossing because there was usually a race meeting at Wincanton Race Course around Bonfire night. Dad would make us a guy and put it in a wheelbarrow and we would it push up the road, where the parked cars were waiting for the gates to open. We would shout out 'penny for the guy'. The luck of the punters on the day or the amount of drink consumed would affect the sum we collected, but we were never disappointed.

When dad wanted to take us to Bath by train for some shopping he would lift us up and the guard would pull us into the carriage and we would go on to Evercreech Junction. We would get off and catch the Pines to Green Park. I remember the guard's compartment always stank of fish. It was a regular thing to carry fresh fish to the various towns along the way for the fish and chip shops. There were also many parcels in the van, so if ever your parcels were fishy, that was the reason why.

Just before 09.00 a train would come up from Templecombe to go onto the branch. The train would stop just past the house and guards like Dickie Bird, Jack Hopkins, Bernard Ware, Les Willsher, Walter (Paddy) Smyth, Reg Brewer, Frank Staddon and Roy Miles would open the door of the luggage compartment and take off three water cans for us. Once or twice a week our family needed a bath. We had no electric or running water and of course it was a problem getting enough hot water for a bath. Dad would carry a tin bath and put it under the step of a passing loco. Drivers like Den Norris or George Morley would open the valve and out would pour our bath water. Mum and dad would carry it in to the house and put it in front of the fire and a family wash would take place. However one morning things nearly went wrong when instead of hot water being discharged, a high pressure steam jet ejected and the bath shot off the sleepers and made its way down the line with father chasing after it.

The down goods off Evercreech would have stopped at the platform at the Junction and the porters would put the three full water cans on the nearside of the buffer beam. The engine, usually a 7F, would then move off travelling steadily on past Lamyatt Crossing and coming to a standstill just before Bruton Road Crossing gates. This goods train was made up of mostly open wagons loaded either with coal from the Somerset coalfields or ballast from the Mendip

quarries. Sometimes a van or two would make up the train together with Shell or Esso oil tanks. None of the train except the engine and the guards van had fitted brakes, so when the train came to a halt, the trucks buffered forward, then steadily rolled back, with the links in the couplings clanging until the train came to a standstill. My father would then reach up high to the buffer beam and lift the water cans off. The 7F would gently take the strain and with maximum power would take the train up the slight bank, over the crossing and make its way on to Cole and Templecombe. What a wonderful sound it made as the trucks started to clunk faster over the rail joints as it gained momentum over the crossing before disappearing out of sight.

The names of the trains are not to be forgotten either. The up Pines would go by at 10.55 returning about 16.10. The Perisher was another heading north about 21.00 loaded with various perishable goods including cattle and sheep. On arrival at the Junction

BR class 4 No.75071 drifts past Bruton Road Crossing with a short passenger train. Mrs. Freda Box, the crossing keeper, can be seen putting the family's washing on the line. (*Keith Barrett collection*)

it would shunt into the middle road and pick up wagons or vans that had been brought up from the branch earlier that evening. The Milky was another train that left Bason Bridge milk factory in the early afternoon with four or five loaded milk tanks. It would head down to Wincanton milk factory, collect another four or five tanks, then go on to Templecombe upper yard where a Southern loco would arrive from the West Country. This train would also come up loaded with milk tanks. It would make up its train with the tanks from the S&D and then be on its way to the pasteurising and bottling dairy at Vauxhall in London, ready for Londoners' breakfasts.

The footplate crews like Wilf Jeans, Ron Merchant, Charlie Hamilton, Len Hardee, Pat Holmes, Albert Manual, Bill Trigg, Ken Atkins and Ian Bunnett were more than generous to the crossing keepers. They would drop the odd lumps of coal off as they were going past. I remember one day when one of the lumps was unusually big and for some reason was very hard. Instead of breaking up, it came like a bouncing bomb and landed very close to demolishing the small shed that housed the telephone and signalling system. Some time later instead of my mother and father doing long shifts, a third keeper, Roy Osborne, was allocated to the crossing. Roy was a regular and he used to stay in the shed which had a circular cast iron coal fire. It was common in the winter to see the fire and chimney red hot and, with the pressurised Tilley oil lamp on as well, it was like an oven inside.

My father, Fred Box, was a gardener, chicken and cockerel keeper, a staunch Labour supporter, on the board at Shepton Mallet prison, a school governor, a Bristol Rovers supporter and sometimes a crossing keeper. His garden was made up in three parts, one on the approach side of the crossing on the up side which also housed the two hen houses; one on the up side just past the crossing house; the other on the down side opposite our house, the same side as the 'Well' used to be. With hens laying plenty of eggs, cockerels being fattened up for Christmas, to be sold to numerous railwaymen on the S&D, there was never a quiet moment. They were fed on a generous diet of the odd cheap bag of feed from the drivers of Jones Mill lorries who drove past the crossing every day. Mother had strict orders not to throw away the potato peelings, but to cook them up and mix them with the Jones chicken meal and feed the fowls, making the most succulent birds you could ever taste.

One day I was at home looking out of the small window that faced towards Cole. I could see smoke coming from an engine from the up line towards the closed gates. I shouted to my mother Freda, 'There's a train coming', but it was too late, the light engine ploughed through the gates. At that time there were four gates, two of which ended up on the buffers, the other two badly damaged. For some time afterwards the road was shut off to the traffic by the means of ropes. When the replacements came, there were no longer four gates but two large ones. They were hung on two massive steel posts that dad thought would be a nightmare to open. They were quite easy, with only two to open, rather than rushing to open four.

I do recall there were certain downfalls with the Bulleids. On one occasion, one of these engines was travelling past the crossing on a bright summer's day in July, hauling a Saturdays only express from the north to Bournemouth. The sparks coming from the chimney set fire to a field of hay,

Parked just below Bruton Road Crossing in 1965 is Dave Box leaning out of the cab of his brother Gerald's lorry, a Bedford 'S' type. (*Gerald Box collection*)

doing extensive damage, not only to the hay but also burning the wooden fence posts alongside the railway, just before the farmer's crossing at Easthill Lane.

Just to finish on the crossing tales, I was at home from school one day when I looked through the doorway from the living room to the front room and saw a glow. I shouted to my mother: 'The house is on fire'. She came running up and shouted to my dad who was in bed asleep at the time. He tried to get down the stairs but the fire was burning too fiercely. The only way was to jump out of the bedroom window, which he did cutting his foot badly on the glass that had been broken from the window. The Fire Brigade was called by using the railway phone to get in touch with Evercreech Junction, who then phoned out on a public line to the emergency services. When they arrived at the crossing they did not realise there was no mains water. The fire started from an open grate we had in the front room. My mother had a clothes horse wrapped around the fire with lots of clothes drying and a spark had jumped out and set them alight. The fire took place around Easter time; we found all our chocolate Easter eggs had melted and also our collection of Airfix plastic planes finished up in unusual shapes.

During one weekend the permanent way gangs were sent to re-ballast the track. The engine crew were from Bath depot, and arrived with a train of open wagons, a works carriage and a guards van headed by a Midland Black 5. I stood by the track for some time watching the gangs lifting the rails by hand. Others packed the sleepers with stone to level the tracks and check the width of the rails. I walked up to the engine and looked at this big loco and was surprised when the driver asked if I would like to come up on to the footplate. At 11 years old I looked up at the height I had to climb to get on to the engine; it was rather daunting. The fireman said 'I will give you a lift up' Although a little nervous of the height, I accepted and was taken on board. I was told to sit on the wooden seat on the opposite side to the driver. The fear was soon put to one side when the ganger's whistle was blown for the driver to move the train forward. The driver responding with a short blast on the whistle and slowly we moved down the track. The driver said: 'Come over my son, sit here and you can have a drive'. I moved across and sat there, regulator closed, but gently running along the track past Lamyatt Crossing. I was told to apply the

steam brake on the engine to stop the train. I think I pulled it too quickly as the driver said 'Careful, because if you brake too fast the men in the wagons will fall over and hurt themselves'.

In March 1960 I left school at 15 and got a job on the S&D as a junior porter at Evercreech Junction. My father said it would be a job for life but little did we know at the time, that within six years all would be gone and dad and I would be looking for employment elsewhere.

I started on the early shift with Bill (Gabby) Pippen and foreman Ern Phillips. I was told that every Monday was brass cleaning day. Amongst the other duties were cleaning toilets, lighting fires in the waiting rooms and stationmaster's office and also looking out for passengers and parcels. Brass cleaning was as important to the station as was the show of flowers that were planted by Ern Phillips and other staff. There was pride in keeping the station looking smart. I was handed a new tin of Brasso and a bar of Bath brick and was shown how to scrape away at the brick with a sharp knife. You made a fine powder that was then mixed with the Brasso into a smooth paste. Then with a cloth it was time to apply it to the many door handles and various other brasses around the station. You were told not to leave any Brasso around the handles as it would turn white and defeat the object of the cleaning. Junior porters on the morning shift started at 07.20, finishing at 15.00 and the afternoon shift started at 14.00 and finished at 21.40.

Vic Freak was a lampman and had a shed at the end of the up platform where he kept all his spare oil lamps and paraffin. His job was to refill all the signal lamps. I admired him for carrying a lamp up the tall signal at the end of the down platform, as it was a long way up. When Ern Phillips retired, Vic was made up to station foreman. Signalman Les Williams would greet me when I went into the South Box at the level crossing end of the station. I would watch the Pines approach the dip between Lamyatt Crossing and the Junction. You would see a puff of steam from the whistle of the loco as the driver would sound on the approaching train. When the Pines was close to the level crossing I would rush up the platform to the front of the train. When it stopped I shouted out in a loud voice 'Evercreech Junction, change here for Glastonbury and Burnham-on-Sea'. Then shout. 'The Pines Express, stopping at Bath, Gloucester, Cheltenham, Birmingham, Burton, Derby, Chesterfield and Sheffield'. One woman asked me to put her three heavy cases on to the train, which I did; she gave me a shilling and asked if I had any change.

On summer Saturdays it was not unusual to see six light engines, safety valves opening with a full head of steam, waiting for their trains to arrive for assistance over the Mendip Hills. The Saturday only specials from Bournemouth, heading North, would be very heavy trains. As soon as they arrived at the platform and stopped, the assisting engine would leave the centre road and be coupled up and ready to depart in minutes. I remember one time when a 4F arrived as the main train loco and the assisting engine was also a 4F. The crews of these trusty steeds were usually from Templecombe, Walt Jeans, Dennis Norris, Rodney Scovell, Ray Stokes, Reg Darke, George Morley, Jack Hix, Keith Barrett, Roy Hix, Alan Hix, Dave (Zippo) Young, Clive Burden, Robin Gould, Bill Trigg, Pete Stoodley and Mervyn Belbin to name just a few.

Signalman Les Williams was a real Somerset cider drinker as were many of the S&D men. Les used to leave work and visit the Railway Hotel next to Evercreech Junction station. After a good session he would then jump on his bike and sing merrily all the way home to Wyke Champflower. At Bruton Road Crossing we could always hear him coming. Passing us he would shout out 'Good night my beauties' and he could be heard singing away in the distance. One night his singing stopped abruptly, so I jumped on my bike and went to see if he was alright. To my surprise there was the rear light of his bike in the grass. Les was in a large patch of stinging nettles, I helped him up and got him back on to his bike. He shouted out 'Thank-you my beauty' and the singing continued as he made his way home.

Guard Frank Packer was another great character not as a drinker but as a cyclist. He used to ride his tall upright bike to work which was fitted with carbon gas lights. You would open the front of the light, and by putting carbon powder into it and adding water it would create a gas through a jet. You lit it by a match and a powerful beam appeared.

A guard from Highbridge would arrive in the evening with the branch train and wait until the Perisher had departed and then go back to Highbridge with the last train of the day. Ted Christopher or Jimmy Yelling were regularly on this shift. Jimmy would walk into the porter's cabin and go over to the hot coal fired oven and take a couple of raw onions out of his bag. He would put them into the oven and bake them, and

have a good evening feast. Drivers George Wheadon, Charlie Philips, Ronald (Chummy) Andrews and Les Warren would usually accompany them for a brew up or a trip to the Railway Hotel.

Loads of shoes from Clarks at Street were commonplace, also mail bags had to be transferred and the odd calf going to a local market. I will always remember the dog that was sent by rail in a large basket with four or five padlocks, together with a bunch of keys tied on the side. A note was enclosed which said please feed the dog, however I could never see the point of locking the basket with so many locks and then leave the keys for anyone to let the dog loose.

On Wednesdays, a side of bacon would arrive from Bath and I would have to get the station parcel bike from the shed and take the bacon over to Barkel Brothers shop at Ditcheat. The bike had a large basket above the front wheel for carrying the various parcels. It also had no gears, just a very low speed which was attained by pedalling like hell. Thank goodness there were no steep hills from the Junction to Ditcheat. Sometimes Ern Phillips would say, 'Could you go from Ditcheat down to my home at Alhampton and pick up some flowers and bring them back to the Junction'. He had grown them and these went into the various flower borders on the station. It must be mentioned that most stations had a marvellous arrangement of flowers, everyone trying to compete for the coveted Station of the Year Award.

Thursday was an experience after the Pines had gone. It was a walk up to the upper yard to collect wagon numbers off all the trucks in the sidings. On the way up to the yard I walked past the top end of the centre road siding where on some occasions one or two carriages were left for a few days. The numbers of the carriages had to be taken, also I had to climb up into the carriages to see if there was anyone asleep or had used them as accommodation for a day or two. In the past it was not unusual to find someone there. After this exercise it was on to the top yard, maybe walking past Alan Vaughan carrying out some welding to the track or points and having a yarn with him before going to the shunter's cabin for a chat and cup of tea with Malcolm Hatherall, Charlie Vaughan or Tony Carroll. After that I had to take all the wagon numbers at the shunting yard and also note any consignment notes affixed to the clip boards on the various wagons. I then had to take the information back to the station to be checked and sorted. It was not my duty to do

Gerald Box sitting on his Triumph Speed Twin next to Bruton Road Crossing where he lived with his family. He used to go scrambling across local fields around Lamyatt and Wyke Champflower, c.1962. (*Gerald Box collection*)

so but I got into the habit of coupling up some of the fitted wagons that were shunted from the branch into the centre road siding. Usually it was in the evening, when the wagons would be coupled to the Perisher.

One winter's night it was blowing a gale and raining heavily, the Perisher had pulled out of the siding and was out on the main up line. With my oil lamp in the green position I moved it from side to side, signalling to the driver of the branch engine to come on down and couple up to the two carriages. As it touched the buffers I quickly turned my lamp red; the engine, a 0-6-0 Collett, stopped and as usual I shot under the buffers. Just as I started to lift the heavy coupling over the hook there was a loud gush of steam from the engine. I realised that the engine was not close enough to couple up so I put my hand over the brake pipe and the engine gently moved closer and I managed to couple her up. However, with the gushing of the steam I could not see or hear anything. I climbed out from under the engine and to my horror the down goods was coming down the line, only a foot away from me. I went to get out of its way and fell, the train went by my foot with only an inch of clearance. I stayed 'led down' until the goods had passed and then crossed the line and up on to the platform. I got on my bike and went home. I must admit it frightened me to death, not with what had happened, but what might have been.

On arrival at work one morning I was greeted by Bill Pippen and told that our jobs today included the trans-shipping of 10 tons of clay. They were in an open wagon that had a hot bearing and could not travel on to its destination. The wagon had been shunted into the siding at the back of the station building and another wagon had been placed alongside to take the clay. We got out our shovels, removed the tarpaulin sheet off the clay and made a start. Not an easy task as the clay was wet and very heavy. After ten minutes of shovelling we were like snowmen and the more we shovelled the dirtier we got. To make things worse we had to shovel the clay from one wagon to the other. The deeper we got down in the clay the higher the clay had to be lifted over to the next wagon. We drank a lot of tea that day.

Whilst working at the Junction I met a young lady from Horsington. After work on the day shift I would ride my push bike from Bruton Road to Horsington to see her. On numerous occasions after our meetings I would ride my bike down to Templecombe lower yard and meet the guard on the northbound late goods, who would lift my bike onto the guard's van. I would travel back to Bruton Road and if the right driver was on they would drop me off home. Stan Moore or Frank Packer were usually the guards on these occasions.

My days living at Bruton Road Crossing and then as a porter at Evercreech Junction were a very special part of my life. As they say, memories are made of this.

(*right*) Porter Alf Elliott in front of Cole station's fish pond. New pupils waiting to catch the train to Sexey's School often had their hats thrown in the pond by the older boys. (*Mick Elliott collection*)

(*below*) Standard class 5 No.73054 stops at Cole with a down local, c.1962. (*Keith Barrett collection*)

(*above*) Senior Templecombe driver Les Cuss leans out of the cab with plenty of steam and smoke for company. (*Ian Matthews collection*)

(*right*) Porter Irving Whittle is seen here in the porter's cabin at Wincanton station in 1962. (*Maurice Whittle collection*)

(*below*) A smashing shot of 4F No.44560 near Wincanton in 1949. Johnny Walker is seen looking out of the cab. (*Keith Barrett collection*)

4F No.44560 stands at Wincanton with a train for Bath. This engine was introduced in 1922 and built for the S&DJR to MR design, c.1963. (*John Cornelius*)

On parade is Standard class 3 No.82002 (82G Templecombe) as it leaves Wincanton with a down local. (*Len Taylor*)

Standard class 4 No.75071 rounds the bend just half a mile north of Wincanton and passes bridge No.132 Verrington Road Bridge with a passenger train for Bath.
(*Len Taylor*)

An unidentified Standard class 4 is seen running towards Verrington Bridge just north of Wincanton station with a down train in the 1960s. (*Len Taylor*)

A stirring action shot of 2P No.40698 with the 13.10 Bath to Templecombe train nearing Wincanton, c.1955. It has got to be one of my favourite pictures. *(E.W. Fry/R.K. Blencowe collection)*

7F No.53803 heaves a long passenger train near Wincanton in 1955. (*E.W. Fry/R.K. Blencowe collection*)

Len Taylor took this wonderful shot of a class 5700 darting through the countryside north of Wincanton. What a breathtaking view it is with the meadows and trees either side of the line. (*Len Taylor*)

(*left*) A 1950s view of SR 2F class G6 No.30274 resting outside the shunter's cabin at Templecombe upper yard. The clock on the outside wall is now in the hands of a private collector. (*Keith Barrett collection*)

(*below*) 2P No.40696 off the road on the catch points at Templecombe. At the back of the loco, from left to right are, ganger Bill Candy, Permanent Way inspector Bernard Curtis and Permanent Way man Fred Foot. In front are Alan Rice (left) and Sid Howe. (*Bob Barnard/Hugh Davies collection*)

(*above*) Driver Johnny Walker (right) and fireman Tony White are seen at Templecombe in the cab of Merchant Navy class No.35028 *Clan Line*, after working a special train up from Bournemouth on the last day of service, 6 March 1966. (*John Cornelius*)

(*right*) In front of class 2 No.41296 are Templecombe railwaymen, from left to right, Cliff Day (fireman), Arthur Hatcher (driver) and Ernie Cawley (coalman). (*Keith Barrett collection*)

(*below*) Merchant Navy No.35011 *General Steam Navigation* seen at Templecombe in January 1966. She was a very rare sight on the S&D. (*Ian Matthews collection*)

Ian Matthews

My school at Templecombe was next to the Somerset and Dorset Railway and within sight of the station, so it was little wonder that the favourite pastime of the Templecombe children was trainspotting. If we were not hanging over the playground wall collecting numbers, we were playing trains *in* the playground, such was the effect the railway had on us. The railway had an effect on the school as well. The school assembly was at 09.00 every morning and prayers would often coincide with the joint departure of the 09.05 train to Bath and Bournemouth. (This was the only train that regularly combined departures to the two destinations, between the station and No.2 Junction). Two long whistles, one from each of the locomotives on either end of the train would give notice that it was about to depart. The first engine would pass and then there would be a pause in the noise whilst the coaches drifted by. It was then followed by the rear engine which, because it was not working, would very often be lifting the safety valves. As the engine passed, it was impossible for the headmaster Mr. Perry to be heard above the noise, so there would be a brief pause in the proceedings until it was quiet once more.

At playtime we were always keen to get outside to see the passing of the Pines Express. Unfortunately as it did not call at the station, this could only be viewed at a distance from the end of the big playground as it passed over No.2 Junction. It was very frustrating to be able to see the type of engine, but not be able to get the all-important number. If an engine took water from the tower next to the school, this was guaranteed to bring us all rushing to the fence to watch. A few words would usually be exchanged with the crew, many of whom we knew. If the weather was hot, lessons were sometimes taken outside, but it was very difficult to concentrate when a train was passing and would usually result in us being shouted at by the teacher.

Most of the children went home for dinner in those days, but we would always call at the station on the way back to school to see the up Atlantic Coast Express thunder through.

Many hours were spent on the station during the weekends and holidays. We found it very difficult to understand the strange coded messages exchanged between the station staff about up and down trains. This was very confusing to the young trainspotter, as the up trains were going down the hill and the down trains were going up. It was some time before we found out that all trains go up to London, regardless of the gradients.

It was very interesting watching the comings and goings at the station, there was always something happening. The large size of Templecombe station could be very misleading to some passengers changing trains. With time on their hands they would often ask, was the town centre very far and were there many shops. This would be greeted with childish laughter and a reply that Templecombe was only a village and that there were only a few shops and if it happened to be a Saturday afternoon they would all be shut anyway.

To cab a loco was worth an extra tick in the loco spotters book. On the Southern this was very rare as trains did not stop for long and the drivers did not seem to have time for the humble trainspotter. Now on the Dorset things were very different, much more relaxed and with the added advantage that we knew some of the crews. One of my friends was Nick Stokes, whose father was driver Ray Stokes. If Ray was taking a light engine back to the shed we could be in for a real treat with a cab ride out to Horsington Crossing and back to lower yard. This would involve passing No.2 signalbox, so we would have to be careful to keep out of sight. On arrival at lower yard we would have to climb out of the cab on the opposite side to the office, again being careful not to be seen. This was really something to boast about to our mates.

Sometimes if we were allowed to help one of the porters with a loaded barrow, we would go across the board crossing at the west end of the platforms. We were very impressed with the ease with which the porters handled the loaded barrows, as we could not get them to move even when they were empty. However, I do recall that in their attempts to get the loaded barrows up the platform ramp, it was necessary to build up momentum going down the other ramp. This did have sometimes disastrous consequences when they got it wrong and the contents of the barrow would be deposited over the crossing and on to the track. Porters that I recall were Len Rose, Ron Mortimer, Don Garrett, Bert Davis, Ron Perry, John Polden, Dave Rendle, Charlie Robinson, Ron Fudge and Frank Styling.

There was another board crossing near the footbridge; this was definitely out of bounds to anyone but railwaymen, as you had to jump down from the platform to go across here.

The bookstall run by Leonard Fudge kept us up to date with the latest spotter's books which were purchased as and when enough pocket money was available. A free drink of water was always available in the buffet, as long as we didn't make a habit of it. Doris Longman was the manageress; other ladies who worked there were Winnie Hannam, Margaret Chant, Joan Miles and Dolly Sanger.

The 64-lever signalbox at the western end of the island platform controlled all the movements in and out of the station on the Southern and on the Dorset. A visit to this very busy control centre could be very interesting; signalmen who were there at that time were Harry Bowles, Eric Knight, Stan Flood, George Hitchcock, Ron Wiffin and Arthur Griffin.

On a cold day the waiting room on platform 2 was a good place to be, as it had a door out onto platform 3 as well. We had to keep an eye out for the station inspectors, as they had an office next door. We didn't have much trouble from Bill Newman, the stationmaster, or inspector Bill Fishleigh, but the other inspector, Bert Moody, was less tolerant of trainspotters. On the Dorset platform there was a great deal of coupling and uncoupling of locomotives as all trains to and from Bournemouth had to have a pilot engine attached for the trip to and from Templecombe Junction. This was undertaken by shunters Stan Matthews, Reg Day, Ron Cox, Joe Coward, Bill Hodges, Jim Cull and Bill Butler.

Every opportunity was taken to visit the station. My mother ran a book club and many parcels would come by rail. If one was expected she would have no problem in getting me to go to the station to collect it, first to the parcels office, where you were likely to see Les Hoskins or Ernie Hooker. Next door in the ticket office would be Ken Stokes or Fred Harper. Then to the goods shed office where you would be greeted by Fred Brown and the sight of hundreds of parcels in every conceivable shape and size, waiting to be delivered by the railway lorry. Other people usually seen at the station would be ticket collector Cecil Gillman and outside, opposite the main entrance, would be the two taxis, driven by Bill Webb and Bill Watts.

A few years later I took up the hobby of racing pigeons. This would involve putting the birds in a pigeon basket and taking them on my newspaper bicycle to the station. They were then sent down the line to be liberated for a training flight. On my return from school it was back to the station to collect the empty basket. On Friday evenings the pigeons were again taken to the station but this time they were put in the Blackmore Vale Flying Club's baskets and sent down the line to be released for the race back to the loft. The carriage and wagon sidings were also worth a visit. If it was winter we used to go in the messroom, where there would be a range fire with a big black kettle boiling on it. If my uncle, Bob Saunders, was on duty we would get a cup of tea and the chance to sit down and engage in some friendly banter with Les Davis, Bob Target, Den Foot, Ian White, Stan House and Roy Mortimer. This was also handy in the winter when snow was on the ground as we used to go sledging down the hill behind the mess hut, then pop in for a warm up.

Sometimes there might be a brakevan shunted into the sidings which had a glimmer of a fire left. This would be brought back to life for a warm up, until someone spotted the smoke. We would then all quickly get out and disappear out of sight.

In the latter years of the railway the carriage and wagon staff, whom we knew well, had a motorbike. They used to ride up and down the yard and we used to have a go on it also. We had to make sure we

(*left*) Bill Newman who was the stationmaster at Templecombe between 1953 and 1966. (*Ian Matthews collection*)

didn't go beyond the wagons at the western end, as inspector Bert Moody lived in Lily Lane, which was on the opposite side of the main line. Another interesting pastime in the yard was playing cricket in one of the large-bogie parcel vans. This was played with a soft ball, but it could get a bit hairy at times, with the ball bouncing off the sides in all directions.

Summer Saturdays and good weather would mean trainspotting at the lower platform, Throop Road. Not as interesting as on the station, but as some of the summer Saturday specials on the Dorset did not call at the station this was the best place to view them. In between trains we would look for things to do; sometimes this would involve putting pennies on the line under the Southern main line bridge (No. 153). That way they would hit the walls and be easier to find after the train had passed. Then perhaps we would all have a go at pulling the signal off. This was just on the Henstridge side of the main line bridge, and two of us could do this by pulling the wire by hand. We used to get a bit worried in case the signalman from No.2 saw the signal going up and down.

Sometimes we would venture into lower yard, especially if there were engines stored out of use in the siding nearest the road bridge, usually a 2P or a 3F. We would climb aboard and after deciding who was the driver and fireman, we would drive the engine to Bath or Bournemouth without moving an inch, great fun.

It was at times like this that we would puzzle as to why some of the engines were fitted with water scoops. Everyone knew that there weren't any water troughs on the Dorset. Also, when returning from overhaul, why did they put those warning flashes on the engines? Did they not realize that there weren't any electric overhead cables on the Dorset. Simple questions for young trainspotters to ponder.

The main street through Templecombe was dominated by two railway bridges and these were involved in a game we used to play. The object was to get the ball over the southernmost bridge. This bridge not only carried the double track main line, but the two platforms as well. The bridge also had very high sides, which we were never tall enough to see over when on the platform. It took quite a swing to get a ball over and down between the two bridges. This game was usually brought to an end by one of the station staff looking over the bridge and telling us off. You would probably get run over if you tried it today.

The bridges were always a favourite around bonfire night as a banger or a rook scarer let off under them could always guarantee a very loud bang.

During 1957 a new secondary modern school was opened at Wincanton and all the children over 11 years old from Templecombe had to travel to Wincanton by train. Unfortunately by 1960 when I started, the powers to be decided that any new starters would have to travel by bus. What bad luck! However, occasionally we used to miss the bus on purpose, and being so keen to get to school, we used to go to the station and catch the 09.05 train and get to school a little late. This did backfire on us a couple of times. One day we were hiding up Back Lane (now called Vine Street). Unbeknown to us, some other boys were hiding up the Main Road towards the hospital. After the school bus had left seven boys suddenly appeared. We had no choice but to catch the train and on arrival at school we were sent to the Headmaster's office to explain why we had all missed the bus. "Well it went early, didn't it", was the explanation.

Another time we were just departing from the station on the 09.05 when we saw the school buses coming back down Church Hill. When we arrived at Wincanton station we found out that the school heating had broken down and everyone had been sent home. So we went over the footbridge and caught the train back home again.

Most of the boys in Templecombe had an ambition to work on the railway, including myself. By the time I left school in the summer of 1964 the writing was on the wall for the railway and I had to look elsewhere for a career. This resulted in me taking up the position of an apprentice carpenter with Wincanton Rural District Council, whose workshops were right next to the railway line, just south of Hawkers Bridge, so I was still able to keep an eye on the trains. I got a lift to work on the back of a motorbike but sometimes had to travel by train, if the lift was not available. Little did I realize that 26 years later I would go some way to fulfilling my original ambition of being a train driver by being a volunteer driver on the Gartell Light Railway near Templecombe and driving 2ft-gauge trains on the old Somerset and Dorset line.

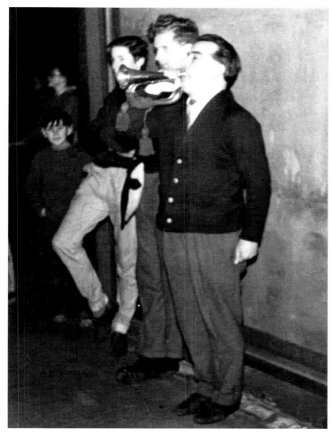

(*above*) Pat Dorland, landlord of *The Royal Hotel*, sounds The Last Post for the final S&D train at Templecombe. Ken Flood also features in the photograph. (*Ian Matthews collection*)

(*above*) Six very smart members of the station buffet staff at Temple-combe in the 1920s. Over the years I wonder how many cups of tea the ladies poured for the thirsty railwaymen and passengers. Note the gas lamps in the background. (*Ian Matthews collection*)

(*left*) Ivatt LMS 2-6-2T class 2 No.41307 intro-duced in 1946 is the back drop for the three railwaymen. From left to right. Leo Elkins, Ernie Cawley and Maurice Miles. (*Ian Matthews collection*)

(*left*) Bill Lawrence, aged 14, in his refreshment uniform (note the cap badge) outside Templecombe signalbox. Bill went on to give 40 years service to the railway and ended up as a Permanent Way inspector, c.1920s. (*Ian Matthews collection*)

(*above*) Bill Lawrence and two Templecombe refreshment room ladies sitting on a parcels trolley, c.1920s. (*Ian Matthews collection*)

(*below*) Railwayman Walter Webb stands proudly at a snowy Templecombe yard with his grandchildren Andrea Howcutt and Jeremy Webb, c.1965. (*Gordon Webb*)

(*below*) Was it really 78 years ago that this picture was taken of staff at Templecombe? Left to right are Jack Wright, Art Langdon, Len Marshall and Walt Legg. (*Ian Matthews collection*)

(*above*) Inside Templecombe signalbox looking west. This box was opened by the SR in 1938 as part of the re-building of the ex L&SWR upper station and superseded the older L&SWR 'A' box and the S&D 'B' box (closed in 1933). The box is constructed in the contemporary Odeon style with rounded ends and big windows. It's 13.45 and the signalman is expecting a train whilst his mate looks on, c.1939. (*S.C. Townroe/R.K. Blencowe collection*)

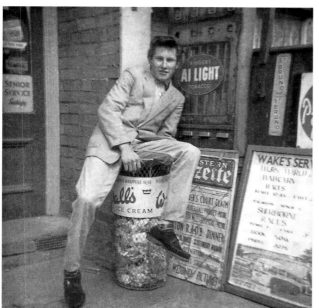

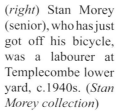

(*left*) Passed cleaner Mervyn Belbin, aged 17, outside Den Mullett's paper shop in Templecombe. The 1950s fashion gives the date away. (*Keith Barrett collection*)

(*right*) Stan Morey (senior), who has just got off his bicycle, was a labourer at Templecombe lower yard, c.1940s. (*Stan Morey collection*)

Stan Morey

I started at Templecombe Motive Power depot as a cleaner soon after my 15th birthday in 1947, a day I had looked forward to for a long time. Most of the workforce, like George Williams, Dick Isaacs, Jack and Sam Hix, Bill Prior, Ernie and Len Hardee and Bill Candy, were known to me as I had spent many hours at lower yard where my father Stan was a labourer. I was soon to learn that lower yard was a den of practical jokers. One had to have eyes in the back of one's head, particularly during winter months when traffic was light and there were more engine cleaners on shed. It was not unusual to get an oily rag at the back of one's neck, of course with everybody showing an air of innocence. On one occasion all of us cleaners had descended into the cabin for our lunch break, leaving Ken Froud washing his hands in the stone sink in the engine shed. It was expected that Ken would be the next to enter the messroom. A bucket of greasy water was placed on top of the messroom door. Unfortunately the next entrant was shed foreman Ken Anderson who received a soaking and a bang on the head. At the time he said nothing, he went home to the top of Slades Hill to change his clothes. When he came back his annoyance knew no bounds, it seemed as if all cleaners were living on borrowed time. After that nobody stepped over the mark for a long time. Many victims of practical jokers in lower yard were not pleased to retrieve their bicycles from the bike rack only to find their front wheels padlocked to the rack. Another favourite joke was when engine drivers with metal lunch boxes left them on the messroom table where they were likely to find them nailed to the table.

Stan Morey (left) and Sam Elkins on a BSA motorbike after a day's cleaning at Templecombe in 1948. (*Stan Morey collection*)

One of many stories that emerged from lower yard was about lady cleaners employed during World War Two. Coming off shift on a very cold late night Arthur Hatcher was looking forward to a nice cup of hot, steaming tea in the messroom. Looking through the window Art could see the lady cleaners hogging the messroom fire. He was not amused as this was a regular occurrence, so he decided to stop it continuing. He climbed on the messroom roof with a bucket of water and tipped it down the chimney. One can imagine the coughing and spluttering, and the ladies covered in white ash. They soon emerged for fresh air and the story went that they did not hog the fire again.

After a period of time I became a fireman, my favourite shift being the night goods out of Poole yard which always had 55 wagons and a brakevan. We picked up the loco for the turn at No. 2 Junction at Templecombe after exchanging with the Bath men at 19.15. By the time we were ready to leave Poole the firebox seemed to have more ash than fire. Coal was almost down to wet slack and it was almost impossible to build a good fire. At the time my first regular driver was Vic Williams and his pride would never allow me to clean the fire. I was lucky that I had Vic as my driver, he was a fine engineman and very considerate on the regulator. Of all the times we worked together on the night Poole, only once did we stop for a few minutes at the top of Broadstone Bank, to recuperate a drop of water. On this trip I was hoping to fill the boiler, but my wishes were shattered when Vic decided one inch of water was enough to proceed. I was hoping to recover more with a regular stop at Blandford Forum, but no such luck. Vic decided not to stop and keep the train rolling. We did stop for a quick splash at Sturminster Newton.

I always looked forward to trips to Bath as a treat as they served Brain's pork pies in the buffet. You would put them on the back of the clack box to warm them, very enjoyable. Other titbits you put there to cook were potatoes and onions (what a smell). My favourite was bacon and eggs cooked on the shovel and if you were at Evercreech Junction you could pick some mushrooms in the nearby fields. A story I recall about mushrooms at the Junction was when the foreman Vic Freak saw a driver picking a big bag of mushrooms. After he picked them Vic went up to him and told him that they had just sprayed the field with insecticide. The driver immediately throws them to the ground. As the driver left for Bath,

Vic has the bag in his hands and with a big grin shouts out: 'Thanks for picking some mushrooms for me'.

On my first trip on a West Country we were working a holiday special from Bournemouth West to Bath Green Park. My driver, Tom Kesteven, could not get the hang of the steam reverser. We spent the trip not much above 45% cut off. The firing shovel didn't get much rest, and matters were not improved by my inability to use the steam firehole door operation. It was a hot summer's day and it was like working in a Turkish bath. I was very pleased to see the top of Masbury. After disposing of our mount at Bath, we enjoyed a comfortable ride back on the cushions.

The night banking turn was one to test the thickest of skins. It was all right working up the bank, but on the return trip down the bank, tender first in the middle of winter with a strong wind coming in from the channel, one was frozen to the marrow.

Many times I have read of people quoting the prowess of locomotive handling by drivers on the S&D. To support this, brings one occasion to mind. On this day our turn was the 11.40 from Bournemouth West, our loco No. 44557 with 6 bogies on as the load – no mean feat for a 4F to keep time, as the timing of the 11.40 was faster than the Pines Express. We left Branksome shed with only one gauge glass and no spare available. On leaving Bournemouth, just past the signalbox our one gauge glass exploded with a loud bang. My driver seemed unperturbed by this setback, thinking that we would get some sort of loco exchange at Poole, but this was not to be. At Poole my driver ran to the signalbox to inform control of the situation. He got back on the footplate, received the green flag and headed for what, for me, was a very worrying trip. It was obvious we were not going to try to keep time as water was scarce all the way. Blandford was reached some 12 minutes behind and 20 minutes at Templecombe No.2, where we were relieved to see a fitter get on the footplate and fit a new gauge glass, to reveal ½ a boiler of water. Throughout the trip my driver took every chance to smile at me and say: 'We shall be all right, mate'. His encouragement to me was

paramount. My driver was Lou Long, a lovely man to work with, and I was privileged to know and work with such dedicated men.

After I returned from National Service I was disappointed to find Vic Williams was no longer my driver, as he had been promoted to assistant deputy foreman. In his place was Tom Kesteven with whom I spent many happy hours. Tom was transferred from Crewe shed to Templecombe. Tom used to tell me about the open market in his home town of Sandbach. He was a good engineman who liked his scrumpy. On one occasion, working an evening goods train from Highbridge to Evercreech Junction, he was the worse for wear from the intake of scrumpy. I insisted he sat on the fireman's seat and I would take over the driving to Evercreech, which scared the living daylights out of me. Whilst I was driving the train across the levels Tom was singing hymns to me. He was a very good organist and was the resident maestro at Horsington Parish Church. On arrival at the Junction I continued to do the shunting while Tom slept it off in the down side shunter's cabin.

As young men, a favourite pastime was to catch the late afternoon passenger train on a Saturday to Bournemouth West. We would ogle the pretty girls and visit a few public houses and enjoy some bottles of beer. Then catch the 22.00 train back to Templecombe.

I worked on the S&D for eight years with fellow railwaymen Basil Foot, Ron Hatcher, Fred Gray, Maurice Miles, Norman Light, Walt Webb, Doug Bernard and many more. A wonderful set of people who weren't just workmates but friends who would do anything for you.

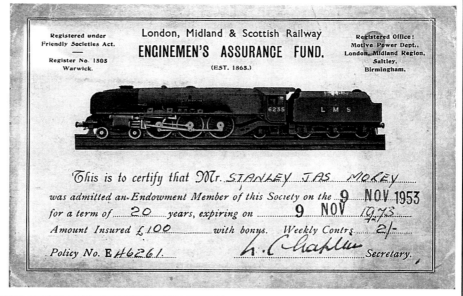

(*above*) This view shows Templecombe No.3 (S&D) platform, c.1905. Note the 17-gallon milk churns. (*Ian Matthews collection*)

(*below*) It looks hard work as Vic Whitlock (right) and Bill Goddard turn 3F No.43194 on the Templecombe turntable. Other men who remember aching joints at the turntable include, Keith Barrett, Norman Light, Wally Arnott, Steve Collins, Gordon Hatcher and John Dray. (*R.K. Blencowe collection*)

LMS 2MT No.41208 blows off steam impatiently at Henstridge, while waiting for a few passengers to join its train, the 12.31 Templecombe to Bournemouth West. It was taken on my birthday, 29 March 1965 (unfortunately not the year I was born). (*Paul Strong*)

(*above*) Driver Fred Fisher and his son Andrew on Henstridge station, three months before closure. Andrew couldn't follow his dad onto the S&D, but he did the next best thing; he produces videos of the old line and preserved railways. (*Fred Fisher collection*)

(*above*) Fireman Ron Hatcher leaving his house to go on duty at Templecombe in the 1950s. (*Ron Hatcher collection*)

(*below*) Henstridge station looking towards Bournemouth. Note the hand crane on the platform. (*Keith Barrett collection*)

(*left*) Standard 4 No.75073 hauls a variety of freight through Henstridge in June 1965. Note the wild flowers on the bank. (*Paul Strong*)

(*below*) An excellent view of 4F No.4169 with a passenger train coming under Landshire Lane Bridge (No.161) on the Somerset and Dorset border, c.1948. (*Keith Barrett collection*)

(*above*) Signalman Alan Cox looks out of the window from the 18-lever signalbox at Stalbridge, which was situated on the up platform, c.1965. (*Paul Strong*)

(*above*) Taken from Stalbridge signalbox on a very murky day, an unidentified Standard draws into the station with a northbound train, whilst signalman Alan Cox looks on to see the changing of the tablet. (*Paul Strong*)

(*left*) Two Standards cross at Stalbridge in 1963 as a number of platform staff look on. Note the very young fireman on the left-hand engine; he looks no more than sixteen. (*Paul Strong*) (*right*) A special train, seen here at Stalbridge, ran over the S&D in 1965 to allow the local MP for North Dorset to see the hardship that would be incurred if the line was closed. The Hymek diesel class 35 No.D7024 was driven by George Welch and the guard was Cecil Martin. It made no difference as the line closed in March 1966. (*George Welch collection*)

(*below*) A super shot of Stalbridge signalbox and station buildings, which includes the stationmaster's house. (*Peter Barnfield*)

Bruce Briant

I started work at Templecombe Lower as a cleaner on just over £6 a week. Men who were there at that time included Trevor and Dennis Nettley, Bert Jones, Percy Hobbs, Walt Jeans, Vic Burt, Bill Silk, Steve Collins, Derek Howcutt and Leo Elkins. After a short time I progressed to a passed cleaner. One day on a special working as a passed cleaner (having done 273 firing turns), my driver Ben Dyer and I rode on the cushions to Bournemouth West to work an extra train back to Templecombe. Ben being a practical joker said before boarding the train: 'How about making a bob or two to spend on a couple of pints of beer?' He went and took the best bicycle from the bike shed at Templecombe (green Raleigh 3-speed, dynamo) and put it in the guards van. Most enginemen used to walk or cycle to work in those days, not many had cars. 'How much do you think we'll get for it?' he asked. I replied 'I don't know'. I wondered what he was going to do with it, and I couldn't believe he had taken it as it belonged to another driver who was coming back on the cushions from Bournemouth to Stalbridge. Of course he was kidding me, the guard dropped the bike off at Stalbridge so the driver could ride home. There were 28 sets of men at Templecombe when I started in 1961, 12 in the top link (passenger),

12 in the goods link and several in the old man's gang as they called it, which was classed as shunting.

On one trip from Bath to Templecombe, we left Shepton Mallet and were coasting down to Evercreech Junction. I was topping the boiler up ready to dispose of the engine back at Templecombe. The engine was an Armstrong 4F No. 44272 which had double nuts on the gauge glasses which meant the water level would be higher than you would expect. The result was, on a falling gradient of 1 in 50, a full head of steam. The engine lifted the water level so high that the brakes went on and we stopped, only to get going again with the large ejector open to get the brakes off. Another time, having arrived at Highbridge with the 08.20 from Templecombe with 2219, we watered the engine, cleaned the fire and made up the fire in the back of the box to keep the engine quiet until our departure with the 14.20 back to Templecombe. The fire had been made up with heavy Welsh coal which was slow burning compared with North coal. We left the footplate for a brew in the cabin with 80lbs of steam and a full glass of water. At 14.00 we came out to take the engine back to Templecombe; we still had 80lbs of steam and a sticky black mass as an apology for a fire. I turned the

Fireman Stan Morey with a flower in his hat, picked from Sturminster Newton station gardens. He is seen here with the local milk train near Stalbridge in 1947. The driver of the 4F No.44102 was Ted Montague, nicknamed 'Doctor', because he carried a doctor's bag around with him. (*Stan Morey collection*)

blower on and tried to liven up the fire with the dart, bent bar and pricker, but with not much success. We never had more than 160lbs of steam and often less all the way to Wincanton. In fact I never put any coal on the fire for the journey from Highbridge to Templecombe. On arriving back, we had enough fire to return back to Highbridge. The crew who relieved us had to get rid of the boxful of fire within two hours of pilot work. The driver Steve Collins and I left the footplate and disappeared quickly in the direction of the loco shed, the sound of the pilot engine blowing off (for the first time since we left Highbridge) ringing in our ears.

I remember a turn when we were on the 16.05 Templecombe to Highbridge. The guard blew the whistle for the right away and off we went around the curve and out of the station. I called out to the driver: 'Stop, we've left the train behind'. The train had run in as the 14.20 from Highbridge. We had walked from the shed to the station to take over the pilotman's engine as they had relieved the men off the Highbridge train engine. The pilotman thought I would be hooking up the train and I thought that the shunter had done it. Of course nobody had done it, no wonder we got the vacuum brake quick.

The winter of 1962/63 was a headache for the operating department. I lived near the lineside just outside Wincanton. One particular week I never saw so many trains running from Templecombe to Evercreech Junction and back, the line was blocked northwards from Evercreech. On the following Sunday two locomotives and eleven empty trucks left Templecombe for the Mendips and spent all day in the hills, whilst men shovelled snow into them. It was one of my very few Sunday turns.

Unfortunately in September 1962 the last through trains from the North were either re-routed or did not run any more. The S&D was slowly being run down, with only three-coach sets being the norm. In January 1966 when the Dorset should have closed, the withdrawal of a replacement bus service allowed the line to continue for a further three months. On one special I worked on in January 1966, we double headed a trip to Highbridge with two Ivatt Tanks. On arrival at Highbridge we uncoupled from the train and moved forward across the WR main line. As we went over the crossover we came to a standstill, a coupling had parted and the brake pipe pulled apart. We held up the traffic on the WR line and by the time we were able to move again, we were not very popular. I suppose without meaning to we were getting a little of our own back on the Western Region. Within three months the S&D was no more than a memory. So ended a happy time for me on the Somerset & Dorset Railway.

An elevated view of 5MT No.2890 (nicknamed 'Crab') near Stalbridge in the 1940s. It looks like fresh ballast has just been laid by the permanent way gang. (*Keith Barrett collection*)

(*left*) Standard class 3 No.82039, with plenty of smoke to spare, storms away from Hammoon overbridge with the 16.45 Bailey Gate to Templecombe Milky. Driver Leo Elkins is seen leaning out of the cab. (*Keith Barrett collection*)

(*below*) On a fine crisp morning 2P No.40601 ambles through the countryside with a short passenger train near Sturminster Newton. (*Keith Barrett collection*)

BR class 4 No.75023 brings in a passenger train for Bournemouth. The focus of attention on the platform at Sturminster Newton is the couple enjoying a cuddle in the shelter. Ted Drew was a stalwart at this station for many years. (*Roger Holmes/ Hugh Davies collection*)

(*below*) This grand old lady, seen at Sturminster Newton station, was built by Vulcan Foundry in 1866 as No.19, later changed to No.15 in 1871. In 1891 her final number was 15a and it was withdrawn in 1914. Note the woman on the right in period dress and the signs for Weymouth and Wimborne. (*Keith Barrett collection*)

(*left*) Guard Roy Miles, looking very smart, was one of life's gentlemen. He was a guard on the S&D for many years and was well liked and respected by his fellow railwaymen. (*Lesley Miles collection*)

London and South Western Ry.

787

TO.

STURMINSTER NEWTON

Via

(*below*) I take great pride in trying to put people's names to pictures but unfortunately I have failed on this occasion. This distinguished array of railwaymen was taken at Shillingstone in the 1920s. (*Keith Barrett collection*)

(*right*) Who is this Somerset and Dorset Railway porter? I would love to know. He is either holding a piece of paper or could it be a very large tip from a generous customer? (*Keith Barrett collection*)

London and South Western Ry.
787
TO
SHILLINGSTONE
Via

(*below*) It is always good to get the names of station staff who made the Somerset & Dorset Railway one of the most popular lines in the country. Here at Shillingstone we have, from left to right, Bert Sherlock (lorry driver), Harold Hooper (signalman), Wilf Savory (porter), Albert Snook (ganger), Don Ridout (booking clerk), Reg Eaton (porter), Ken Davey (stationmaster), Alan Cox (signalman) and Bert Scammell (signalman), c.1965. (*C.L. Caddy*)

Samuel Crane

Fatal Accident at Shillingstone Station

This headline appeared in *The Western Gazette* on 5 January 1912 and the article read as follows:

Quite a gloom was cast over this locality on New Year's Day when it became known that Samuel Crane, a checker, employed at the railway station had died as the result of an accident during the afternoon. The deceased was well known by a large number of the public who travel through this station, and was much esteemed by all on account of his studious attention to passengers and his cheery disposition. He was 41 years of age, and for 23 years had been employed at the station. He was also chairman of the Parish Council. The deceased leaves behind a widow and eight children, the majority of whom are of tender years. The greatest sympathy goes out to them in their terrible bereavement.

The inquest was held at the church-room on Tuesday. George Crane, gardener, of Iwerne Minster, gave evidence of identification, and said he was unaware that the deceased had any illness. He was ordinarily a healthy man. Richard Spencer, of Shillingstone, assistant manager in the coal yard at the station, deposed that he knew the deceased very well, and saw him on the Monday previous to what had occurred. He spoke to him in the yard about one o'clock, when he appeared to be alright in every way. Witness saw the 15.20 up train from Bournemouth to Bath come into Shillingstone station. He also saw the train go out of the station in the direction of Sturminster. After the train had gone he saw Crane on a horse-box, which was at the rear of the train. The deceased was on the off-side footboard of the van, standing up. Witness observed nothing further until he saw Crane lying on the metal. Deceased was riding with both feet on the footboard. So far as witness could see Crane had nothing in his hand. About five minutes had elapsed from the passing of the train, when he looked round and saw Crane lying on the metals. He was lying about 200 yards from the platform in the direction of the archway. Witness went down to him and found him lying face downwards. He was bleeding very much. The metals at the spot were in a V shape. Deceased was clear of the metals on which the train went, and was lying on the near side to the up line. His left arm was slightly extended and his right arm was practically underneath him. He was of the opinion that he pitched on his head. His legs were in a little cramped position. He was unconscious. Witness did not notice where deceased's hat was or whether any of the clothing was torn. He could not say how deceased got from the off to the nearside. The train stopped on the bridge, and witness having been called by a porter, went to the spot. When the train stopped the horse-box began running back down the gradient towards the station. It hadn't then reached Crane on the back journey. When the horse-box first passed witness he believed it was coupled. If that was so Crane must have uncoupled it in transit from the station to the bridge. The body was taken to the station premises and the doctor was called, after which the body was taken home by the foreman. The body was found facing towards Blandford. He did not see the deceased step from the horse-box. By Inspector Biggs: The deceased was clear of the metals but between those on which the train was running.

George Savory, manager of Messrs Smart & Son's coal yard at Shillingstone station, deposed to being called to render assistance. He was in a shed at the time, and on running out he saw the body lying between the metals over which the box had run. When he saw the horse-box coming backwards his intention was to try and pull Crane out of the way. As the horse-box was running back it was gaining speed, the brake not being down. By the Foreman: He assisted in the removal of the body, carrying it on a door.

John Marsh, porter at Shillingstone Railway Station, deposed that five minutes before the accident he was talking to Crane, when he was in good health. The horse-box in question had to be taken off at Shillingstone when the train got up on the bank, generally when the train was stopping. The coupling would be unscrewed before leaving the station, and when the box got to the bridge the coupling had simply to be lifted off. There was no-one, as far as he knew, who could have uncoupled the box but Crane, and in the present instance it must have been done while the train was in motion. It was not unusual to use a shunting pole to uncouple passenger trains. If Crane had successfully uncoupled the box while the train was in motion there would have been no need for him to have got off the horse-box. Where he was found was near where the uncoupling would ordinarily take place. When he saw the body on the line he shouted to the signalman to divert the box, and then rushed up to render what assistance he could. By the Foreman: He saw nothing on the footboard which would cause the deceased to slip.

Thomas Hardacre, of Bath, the driver of the train to which the horse-box was attached, said the train arrived at Shillingstone at the right time. He had to leave a horse-box at Shillingstone, having picked it up at Blandford. Crane came up and told him there was one off on the bank. He eventually ran out to the bank and stopped as was customary. He knew the spot where Crane's body was found. It would be about 30 or 40 yards from the tail end of the train. When Crane fell the train could not have been going very fast. The trains were generally stopped before any uncoupling took place. Crane gave witness the signal to stop and then witness lost sight of him. He presumed it was Crane who uncoupled the box as there was no-one else about. By the Foreman: He had the signal to stop from Crane, and re-started on the authority of the guard with a flag. It was not the practice of the person uncoupling to give the guard the right away. Before he re-started he could see that the horse-box was clear.

Robert Ames, stationmaster at Shillingstone, deposed to having seen the horse-box. The wooden step on which Crane was standing was dry and in proper order. The rear and front couplings were also alright. By the Foreman: The steps on the end of the box were only used to get to the roof lamps.

Dr. Newbould, of Childe Okeford, deposed to having previously attended Crane for neuralgia in the arm, but nothing of an organic nature. Apart from that he was an ordinarily healthy man. On Monday afternoon he was sent for by Mr. Ames and saw deceased in the shed just after four o'clock. He was bleeding from both ears and witness formed the opinion that he had fractured the base of the skull, and that the brain was lacerated. There was also a compound fracture of the left forearm. There were injuries on both sides of the head, but the injury on the right side was the most severe. He was of the opinion that the injury must have been caused by the train, rather than by a fall. There must have been some direct violence to knock him on the head like that. It was quite probable that the couplings might have come in contact with his head, and that the injuries to the arm were caused afterwards by the wheel of the box going over it. Deceased lingered until five minutes past six. Witness was with him practically the whole time. The case was hopeless from the first.

At the request of the jury the guard of the train, Abraham Hamblin, was called. In reply to the Coroner, he said the screw coupling was undone at the station and left on until the bank was reached, when it was lifted off. The train stopped in due course, and the box beginning to run back he gave the right away with his flag. The uncoupling must have been done by Crane, as there was no-one else there to do it.

Before summing up, the Coroner said all of them knew Samuel Crane, who, he believed, was held in the highest respect by everybody, and was generally liked. His untimely death was a matter for deep regret, not only to the station staff, but also to the villagers, and also to the travelling public of which he was one. It was a sad accident, especially coming as it did at the start of a new year, and must be a terrible blow to those who were near and dear to him. Proceeding, the Coroner said the duty of the jury was to ascertain the cause of death, and whether there had been any negligence on the part of anyone. So far as the evidence went he was unable to see that the accident was attributable to negligence on the part of anyone, everything having been done with due regard to the regulations of the Company. A point had been raised as to whether the guard of the train ought not to be satisfied that everything was alright before proceeding, but as that had nothing to do with the cause of death, it did not arise there. If it did it would be a point in favour rather than otherwise, as the train was going away from the horse-box and not proceeding towards it. It seemed to him that nothing had been done which ought not to have been done. The train left the station with the deceased riding on the step of the horse-box, which was duly uncoupled. Deceased was seen to give the signal for the train to stop for un-coupling, and then probably what happened was the poor fellow fell and, no doubt his head came in contact with some part of the train. He advised them, if they were satisfied, to return a verdict that the occurrence was accidentally caused.

The jury retired for a short deliberation, and on returning into the Court said they were unanimously of the opinion that the deceased came by his death accidentally, whilst in the discharge of his duties, and that none of the officials or railway staff were in any way to blame. The jury also expressed their sincere sorrow and sympathy with the widow and children, and desired that their fees should be given to them.

Mr. Ames said on his own behalf, and that of the staff he desired to express the deep regret they all felt at the sad loss they had sustained. During the 18 years Sam had been under him he had found him to be a good servant, honest, straightforward and a good workman.

Chief Inspector Biggs said he desired on behalf of the Railway Company, whom he represented, to express the deepest sympathy with the bereaved widow and children.

(*right*) On a very dismal day WC class No.34105 Swanage, is approaching Shillingstone with an express for Bath. (*Keith Barrett collection*)

(*left*) With a view of the beautiful countryside of Dorset, we observe 7F No.53809 (now preserved at Butterley) leaving Shillingstone with a down passenger train. (*Keith Barrett collection*)

(*right*) With railway maintenance always in the news, how nice to see the immaculate condition of the track and ballast work, carried out by the S&D permanent way gang at Stourpaine and Durweston Halt. (*C.L. Caddy*)

(*left*) LMS 2P No.696 with a down passenger train on the short level stretch north of Milldown, Blandford. The train is a three-coach ex-LSWR corridor set, two strengtheners and a van, c.1936. (*Richard Dagger collection*)

(*right*) S&D Bulldog No.62 with a train near Blandford, c.1900. She was built at Derby Works in 1896, renumbered LMS No.3194, then BR No.43194 and withdrawn in 1960. (*Jack Hobbs collection*)

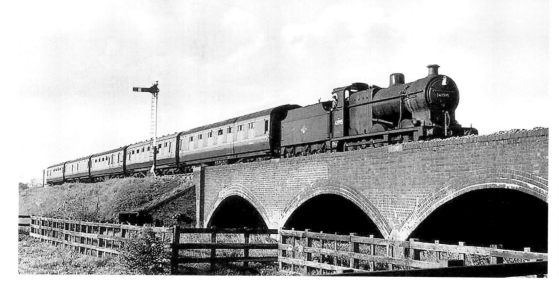

(*left*) A striking picture of 4F No.43995 crossing the River Stour just south of Blandford Forum. (*Keith Barrett collection*)

BR class 5 No.73051 is about to leave Blandford with a Bath train. The porter on the platform looks like Nobby Whiting. (*C.L. Caddy*)

Having run round its train, Standard class 4 No.80067 is seen coupling back on to the rear of its train at Blandford ready to return to Templecombe in 1965. (*C.L.Caddy*)

Heavy snow at Blandford Forum in January 1963 with the 12.18 to Bournemouth pulled by 4F No.44411 on the left. On the right is 4F No.44417 which will form the 12.35 goods to Templecombe. (*Graham O'Donnell collection*)

Ivor Ridout with shunting pole in his hand carries out some shunting at Blandford Forum with 7F No.53806 in attendance. (*Keith Barrett collection*)

(*left*) A different type of motive power with a 1921 left-hand drive model T Ford imported from U.S.A. Eric Wilfred Smithers is standing proudly by this classic vehicle. This T9 was seen delivering goods near Blandford station in 1927. Eric's son Graham trained at Blandford camp and often travelled on the S&D. Nice to have a family connection to the photograph. (*Graham Smithers collection*)

(*right*) Schoolboy Graham O'Donnell (his grandfather Walt Warren is seen below in charge of the Scammell) is enjoying being on the footplate of Ivatt class 2 No.41296 at Blandford. The engine was heading the Bailey Gate to Templecombe milky, c.1959. (*Graham O'Donnell collection*)

(*left*) Driver Walt Warren with his British Railways Scammell, known as the mechanical horse. It is seen here en-route to its base at Blandford with a load of hurdles. (*Graham O'Donnell collection*)

106

(*above*) 7F No.53808 is seen at Charlton Marshall heading north with a LCGB Rail Tour in 1962. (*Keith Barrett collection*)

(*below*) A view of LMS 2P No.40697 taken from the platform as it stops with a down passenger train at Spetisbury Halt in 1950. (*R.K. Blencowe collection*)

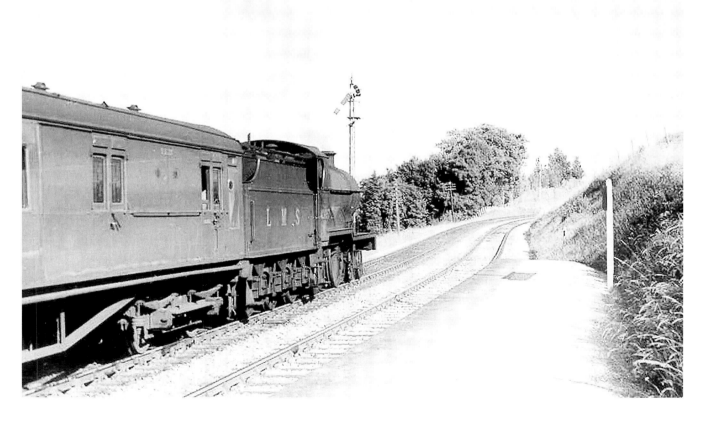

(*left*) Standard class 4 No.76026 waits to leave Bailey Gate on an up train. In the background is the United Dairies' Milk Processing Factory, formerly Carter's and Dorset Modern Dairies. (*Keith Barrett collection*)

London and South Western Ry. 787
TO
BAILEY GATE
Via

(*right*) George Pitman stands in his full stationmaster's uniform on the platform at Bailey Gate. (*SDRT collection*)

(*left*) On a very sunny day near Bailey Gate, a local goods train drifts away with a rake of wagons and a brakevan. (*Keith Barrett collection*)

(*above*) Built by Fowler in 1874, No.23 is seen here tender first with a freight at Corfe Mullen in 1912. Note the footplate man with a straw boater. (*Keith Barrett collection*)

(*below*) Getting into its stride is S&DJR No.60 which has just passed Corfe Mullen signalbox with a mixed freight for Wimborne, c.1912. (*Keith Barrett collection*)

(*above*) BR Standard 5 No.73019 winds its way into Broadstone with the down Pines Express on 13 May 1961. (*C.L. Caddy*)

(*below*) S&DJR No.36 approaching Wimborne from Bailey Gate, c.1903, on the old line which closed to S&D passenger trains in 1920 and to goods in 1933. (*C.H. Eden/R.K. Blencowe collection*)

(*right*) Afternoon calm as Standard class 4 No.80147 approaches Creekmoor Halt with the 13.10 Bournemouth West to Bristol Temple Meads train. The SR main Waterloo to Weymouth line can be seen in the background. (*Keith Barrett collection*)

(*left*) 7F No.53810, one of eleven of its class, could do with a day with the cleaners. It is seen here in 1950 at Poole, with fireman Gerald Chant enjoying a rest. (*H.F. Wheeller/ R.S. Carpenter collection*)

(*right*) Driver Ray Stokes leaves Poole with Ivatt class 2MT No.41243 at the head of the 17.30 Bournemouth West to Templecombe stopping train on 13 April 1964. On the left can be seen the Henry Harbin Secondary Modern School and Poole Stadium. (*Keith Barrett collection*)

S&DJR No.20 being serviced on Branksome shed. Built by Fowler in 1874, it was reboilered in 1893 and 1910, then withdrawn in 1928. *(C.H. Eden/R.K. Blencowe collection)*

4-4-0 No.15 passing Branksome with the 07.00 ex-Bath in 1901. It is hard to believe that this photo is 104 years old. (*C.H. Eden/R.K. Blencowe collection*)

(*left*) In this wonderfully evocative photograph, 7F No.53806 emits a volcanic amount of smoke as it leaves Bournemouth West with the 11.12 to Sheffield in 1961. (*SDRT collection*).

(*right*) Guard Alf Metcalfe looking very smart, leaves his home for duty at Bournemouth. (*Ray Metcalfe collection*)

(*left*) On a wet and downcast day S&DJR class 2P No.15 runs into Bournemouth West with a down train in 1913. (*Keith Barrett collection*)

(*above*) Scottie goods No.44 immaculately turned out at Bournemouth West in 1901. A member of the crew is busy with the shovel while his mate is on the tender. (*C.H. Eden/R.K. Blencowe collection*)

(*below*) 0-6-0 No.4557 is seen here at the popular holiday station of Bournemouth West in 1932. (*Keith Barrett collection*)

Photographed from under the A37 road bridge adds a pleasing touch to the idyllic setting at Pylle. (*R.E. Toop*)

(*above*) On a misty day in May 1965, class 2 No.41307 with the 09.55 Evercreech Junction to Highbridge train, is approaching Pylle. (*C.L. Caddy*)

(*below*) 3F No.43194 enters Pylle Halt with the 14.20 from Highbridge to Evercreech Junction on 21 August 1958. Even for a small station it had a stationmaster's house and a goods shed which were combined on the down side. (*Hugh Ballantyne*)

(above) A grimy Midland 3F with pre-nationalization number 3464 heads through West Pennard with a rake of wagons for Highbridge. (*Keith Barrett collection*)

(*below*) LMS Johnson class 1P No.58072 showing a Highbridge shed code 71J wanders through West Pennard. Staff who have worked at this station include, Fred Lester, Paul Fry, Cecil Jones, Bert Rhymes, Evelyn Curtis, (who always kept a fresh array of flowers in the signalbox), Reg Biffin and Charlie Ham. (*Keith Barrett collection*)

(*above*) In 1958 an accident occurred at West Pennard when a runaway train known as the Highbridge Market slipped violently on the greasy rails, causing the couplings to snap. Here we can see the goods wagons, which were carrying tinned milk packed in cardboard boxes, on their sides. Fortunately there were no casualties with the crew. (*Keith Conibeer collection*)

(*right*) Signalman Tom Salisbury is about to set off to work at West Pennard on his motorcycle. I hope there is not a wind about as his L plate doesn't look very secure. Note the horn, that would certainly scare anything in his way. (*Joy Church collection*)

A modeller's delight at Glastonbury and Street station, with the signalbox, canopies, overbridge and platforms. What a pity it is not still there. (*Keith Barrett collection*)

(*above*) 3F No.43194 approaches Glastonbury with an Evercreech Junction to Highbridge service train in 1959. Note the sharp curve of the track shown in front of the gasometer on the left. (*Keith Barrett collection*)

(*right*) Ron Hatcher and Pat Evans are on the footplate of 3F No.43248 as it makes its way under the footbridge out of Glastonbury with a Highbridge to Templecombe passenger train. (*Ron Hatcher collection*)

(*above*) Signalman Roy Davies exchanges tokens with the Highbridge crew of 3F No.43216 at Glastonbury in 1958. (*Keith Barrett collection*)

(*left*) Roy Davies, again with tablet in hand, walks down the stairs of the 29-lever Glastonbury signalbox of Midland appearance. His bicycle is under the veranda and I wonder if the kettle is on for another cup of tea. This was also home for Eric Miles, another signalman. (*Keith Conibeer collection*)

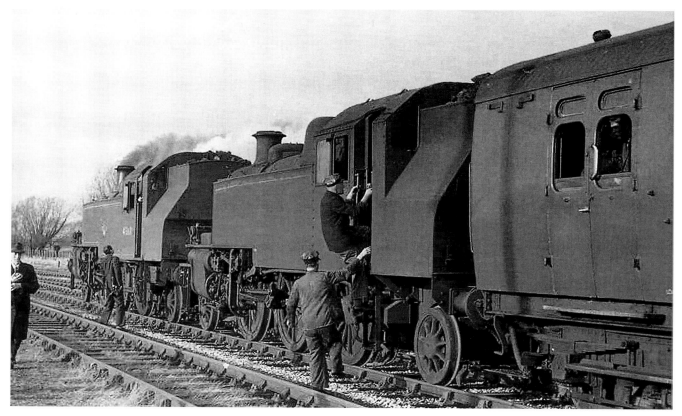

(*above*) Driver Les Cuss and fireman Bruce Briant are seen returning to the footplate at Glastonbury. Two members of the same class, Ivatt Tanks Nos. 41307 and 41283 are working The Mendip Merchantman Rail Tour towards Highbridge on 1 January 1966. (*Keith Barrett collection*)

(*left*) Six members of staff on parade at Glastonbury, who between them have a total of 268 years service working on the S&D. In the picture are Bill Milton, Ralph Poore, Ted Billet, Sam Bailey, Charlie Ham and Stan Ford. (*Paul Fry collection*)

(*above*) 1P 0-4-4 Tank No.58073 arriving at Glastonbury with the 16.15 local from Templecombe to Highbridge. Station foreman Hughie Durston is seen walking towards the ramp leading to the up platform. The flags were out at the station as it was 28 August 1954. It was 100 years to the day since the Somerset Central Railway was opened and a special excursion train was running. (*Percy Parsons collection*)

(*right*) 3F No.43218 approaches Glastonbury with a local train from Templecombe in 1959. Who are the three waving platelayers? (*Keith Barrett collection*)

An Ivatt Tank drifts into Ashcott and Meare with a Highbridge to Evercreech Junction local. *(R.K. Blencowe collection)*

(*right*) Edna and Archie Atwell with their Standard Ten motor car. They both worked and lived at Ashcott station, where this picture was taken. By their side is their faithful dog Spot. (*Janet & Tony Rossiter collection*)

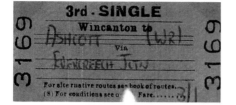

(*below*) The flags are flying at Ashcott on 28 August 1954, as the local residents welcome 3F No.43201. The loco is hauling the special train from Glastonbury to Burnham-on-Sea to mark the Centenary of the Somerset Central Railway. Note Guy Parsons clearing the track of onlookers. Nowadays Health and Safety would have a field day. (*Stan Blacker collection*)

(*above*) A local train approaching Shapwick station in 1964. Fireman Mike Lewis on No.3128 holds out the tablet for the signalman. (*E.T.Gill/R.K. Blencowe collection*)

(*below*) A glorious summer's day sets the scene at Shapwick, as the signalman gives the road to the driver of class 2 No.41214, c.1964. (*E.T.Gill/R.K. Blencowe collection*)

(*above*) A view of Shapwick station looking towards Ashcott. The crossing gates are closed as permanent way men are busy on the right of the photo. This station was a desolate spot, surrounded by wetlands, and was a considerable distance from the village. (*R.K. Blencowe collection*)

(*below*) Fireman Rodney Scovell takes a broadside shot of class 2251 0-6-0 No.3215 as his driver George Welch basks in the sun. (*Rodney Scovell*)

(*above*) 3F No.43204 eases into Edington Junction station with a goods train, whilst driver Dennis Nettley is about to climb on to his engine on the opposite platform, c.1952. (*R. Casserley*)

(*below*) A hive of activity at Edington Junction, c.1946. We have a train coming in from Glastonbury, passengers on the platform and goods wagons in the bay. Note the S&DJR ladder up against the lamp. (*J.W. Sparrowe/R.S. Carpenter collection*)

(*above*) Class 2 No.41307 coasts away from Edington with a mixed train. The station house which is still there today can be seen on the right of the picture. (*Maurice Cook collection*)

(*below*) Class 2 No.41296 races past Huntspill Crossing with a mixed train in November 1964. The crossing was situated between Bason Bridge and Edington. (*Paul Strong*)

(*above left*) Crossing keeper Irene Hynam at Huntspill Crossing where she lived and worked for over thirty years. On the day this photo was taken in 1964 Irene was off duty, but the appearance of an eight-wheeler lorry parked up on the verge with the driver Paul Strong taking photos, was something of an event. Irene came out of the house, offered Paul a cup of tea and he took this photo of her. (*Paul Strong*)

(*above right*) Temporary crossing keeper Walter Clark at Huntspill Crossing, deputising for Irene Hynam. Walter worked on the S&D for many years as a patrolman on the permanent way on the Bridgwater and Highbridge lines. (*Paul Strong*)

(*left*) Driver Stan Bedford is seen on the left with an unknown fireman aboard 3F No.43792, c.1948. Stan was a railwayman all his life, starting at Bath Green Park in 1923. He moved to Evesham in 1936, back to the S&D at Highbridge and then on to Taunton when the S&D closed. (*Barbara Burdge collection*)

Bason Bridge station looking towards Edington. The milk factory can be seen on the left-hand side. Staff who worked at this station included Percy Parsons, John Rice, Edgar Hicks, Reg Slocombe, Frank Jones, Freddie Gas and Cliff Gannicott. (*Keith Barrett collection*)

On a very wet day, Highbridge station is full of churns. Look at the number of staff on duty, as they line up for a photo, c.1920s. (*Norman Ashman collection*)

John Simms

When it came to the 'railway bug' there was never much chance of my avoiding infection. Grandfather Simms was a signalman on the Somerset and Dorset until he retired from Evercreech Junction North in the mid '50s. Uncle Jack drove road delivery vehicles, Uncle Ted signalled until the line closed and aunts Bet and Edna were also employed on the 'Dorset' at different times. Some of their stories have been captured in the previous books by Alan Hammond.

Now the keener-eyed amongst you will have noticed that there is no mention of my father Joe in the foregoing list. He was the exception to the family rule, following a career in the Royal Air Force and the Civil Service. Nonetheless he was well-enough known amongst the S&D 'family' and it is probably safe to reveal more than 50 years after the event that he was riding as an unofficial passenger in the brake of the last train north over the viaduct at Shepton Mallet in 1946 before its collapse.

Two years after this, Joe married my mother Betty in Derby and I made my entrance in 1951. The family residence was in Stanley Common a small mining village, in Derbyshire, and before long I was being taken out and about for pram and pushchair rides and then walks around the area. At this point heredity began to break through as my favourite trips were either along Common Lane to the railway bridge or to the local station, West Hallam for Dale Abbey, on the Nottingham Victoria to Derby Friargate line. This also figured in my Friday lunchtime outing with Grandad Hawley to the colliery by the station to collect his weekly pay, the colliery yard being big enough to have its own shunting locos at work. Visits to *The White Hart* and *The Bateman Arms* on the way back no doubt planted another seed that is still with me.

Of course with the family tree being split between Somerset and the East Midlands the main family holiday each year saw us boarding a train at Derby Midland for Evercreech Junction from whence Uncle Jack would collect us in his Morris 8 for onward transport to Ditcheat. The earliest memory of this journey I have is not of mighty engines or coaches but of the environs of Shepton Mallet. Showerings' premises then had a giant figure of the Babycham deer on the roof and as that swept past the windows it was time to hoist down the suitcases and get ready to alight at the Junction.

But engines began to interpolate into the holiday images. It took no time at all to notice the Bulleid Light Pacifics as being different to anything else I saw and there was a ride home from Bath Green Park behind Jubilee 45570 *New Zealand* that has stuck with me as noisy and memorable (we must have been nearer the engine than usual). We also went on a Sunday excursion from the Junction to Burnham behind a 3F 0-6-0, spending a long time in Highbridge waiting to cross the Western Region line on the level as Swindon-designed machines with copper capped chimneys howled past on the WR side. Sadly my six-year-old self compared this trip to the seaside unfavourably with the other weekly holiday in which the maternal grandparents loaded me into a train at West Hallam for the ride to the Derbyshire Miners' playgrounds at Skegness and Mablethorpe.

Then came 1959. West Hallam Ordnance Depot had closed its clerical section, father was at Chilwell and he disliked it. So he put in for an overseas posting and off we went to Rheindahlen in Germany until 1963. With low-flying jets and lots of other distractions, such as the Cuban Missile Crisis, railways weren't the priority interest of old but the box brownie caught some pictures of Class 64 and 86 Tank engines as we went around Europe and if we paused anywhere near a railway my feet inclined in its direction. 1962 saw us back on leave and father and I went to a field between Evercreech Junction and Cole where I photographed the southbound 'Pines'. A bit disappointed (I was 11 years old, so bear with me) that the engine was 'only' a Standard 5MT (73047 I believe) but the picture came out and the crew gave a smile and a friendly wave.

1963 and we were back for good, taking up residence in Taunton. The rented house in Leslie Avenue was gloomy and depressing but at the other end was the Forty Steps footbridge and it was all of ten minutes walk to the corner of Railway Street where the locospotters of Taunton foregathered for the grandstand view of the west end of the station, the loco shed yard and the goods avoiding line. My leisure time had a dominant theme to the point where the retired railwayman opposite passed a batch of his railway books on to me just before he died. Once again, many thanks Mr. Perkins. I still have your gifts.

We still went to Ditcheat but now by family car and trips to the Junction were by negotiation. Sometimes

I could arrange the journey home via West Pennard and a couple of times the sight of a signal in the 'off' position led to negotiations re 'waiting to see the train'. Each time it was 41296.

With the arrival of loco numbers in these ramblings it should be obvious that I'd succumbed completely to the railway bug and pocket money was saved up for days out chasing the last years of British steam. However I was regarded as something of an eccentric amongst my fellow 'spotters'. Whilst they would aim for busy stations or shed bashing I was quite happy to go to secondary lines. So when the family travelled to Derbyshire I might well go to Derby Midland or to Ilkeston Junction on the Erewash Valley main line but I was equally happy to spend an afternoon at West Hallam where there would be two or three trains an hour. In August 1964 I made my last journey from the old childhood haunt. 43064 took the excursion to Nottingham Victoria and then B1 61141 conveyed us on to 'Skeggy' where there were filthy Ivatt 4MT Moguls, ice cream, the beach and 'The Wild Mouse'. On the way back 61141's fire cast glare onto evening light smoke as we pounded along past Great Northern Railway somersault signals. A month later passenger services ended but freight ran for another four years. Grandad Hawley's pit had already closed, the banging of metal sheets and the wind in the telephone wires being part of the backdrop of sounds at West Hallam station.

But what of the S&D? Uncle Ted was still signalling and by now the writing was obviously on the wall for the line, and for Ted and his fellow 'Dorset' railwaymen which included Ned Ashman, Bert Baker, Cecil Cooper, Reg Staddon, Ronald Dyke, Ted Lambert and Vic Freak. I visited Bath Green Park a couple of times, travelling by train to Spa and then walking across. I can still recall just how quiet Green Park station was between trains. Highbridge always seemed to be haunted by Collett 0-6-0 locomotives, some of which would come to Taunton shed for attention from time to time as Highbridge's remaining repair facilities were run-down. It was a railway almost in limbo although a cycle ride to Glastonbury one Wednesday afternoon in 1965 found an Ivatt 2MT 41290 shunting in the yard, and then departing with an eleven-wagon train giving the working branch line atmosphere with closure only a few months away. Then there was the December '65 bus ride to Glastonbury, another bus to Wells and a walk to Masbury. Along came the train. And the camera jammed. Less than

gruntled I watched the Standard 4MT Tank as it ran into the afternoon and my memories.

Then closure didn't happen. In the half-life of the 'emergency service' of early 1966 I visited Green Park once more. The shed could be walked round easily ... no-one cared enough to boot out wandering 'spotters' with the alacrity of yore ... and lines of cold engines sat awaiting the tow to the knacker's yard. At the station, 82001 waited with three coaches with no crew or prospective passengers in sight. It weighed, even on my teenage spirits, enough to make me shamefully glad to be back at Spa and onto an active and well-loaded train with passengers aboard.

But then it was 5th March 1966. Money considerations meant the day was going to be spent at Highbridge where many crews over the years had worked, like Bernard Andrews, Tony Rossiter, John Baker, Terry Fry, John Lancastle, Billy and Keith Conibeer and Harry Pearce. I boarded the stopping diesel multiple unit from Taunton to Bristol Temple Meads, arriving at Highbridge around 8.00 a.m. This meant that I was in good time to see 41249 shunting milk tanks in the yard and then running through the S&D station with seven in tow en-route to Bason Bridge and the milk factory. It then returned and did some shunting before departing light engine towards Evercreech. Overall, however, quiet reigned and I wandered into the main 'Dorset' building whose doors were open but was deserted. Fossicking about I 'liberated' an LMS Health Insurance poster and then returned to the old excursion platform. 41283 worked the remaining branch passenger service with two coaches (W7366 and W21168) and then more peace descended. Having been joined by another teenage enthusiast we decided to walk up to the old Works and Shed. The 'bobby' in East C box was either dozing or couldn't be bothered any more because we weren't challenged as we made our way in the cess alongside the track to the old engineering heart of the S&D. A look around found quiet dereliction with the bare amount of facilities for basic servicing. We began to walk back.

As we came clear of the lee of the buildings there was a loud bang and the noise of shot sailing not too far over our heads. Most '60s 'spotters' were familiar with the wrath of shed foremen but this seemed a bit strong, especially in the circumstances of the day. A rapid look-around showed a farmer who was engaged in rook shooting and was obviously not used to activity on the line. Mutual alarm allayed, all involved in the incident went on their way.

Two hours elapsed between the departure of 41283 and the next activity, the arrival of 41307 and 41249 with the nine-coach Locomotive Club of Great Britain train for a 55-minute stay in which the day reached its most hectic stage. Both engines ran to the shed to turn with an escorting force performing the gricer gallop along the tracks to get the photographs under the belt.

And then three more hours in which all the activity was on the WR main line as the clock ticked around to the last passenger train of the lot, the 4.20 to Evercreech Junction. Just before this, D7041 worked nine milk tanks to Bason Bridge and then it was the 'moment of glory' for 41249, W7368 and W21168. I had once again walked along the line and photographed it as it cleared the Works area, also having placed an old halfpenny on the line for flattening.

The final walk back to the station was another memorable one. As I reached the end of the platform a terrier in ill-humour appeared and went for my ankles. No flesh was punctured but the hole in the jeans was going to take explaining when I got home. When it came to visiting locosheds I decided that I preferred to take my chances with railway staff in future rather than take on shot and canines.

Next day, 6th March, Father and I set off by car to Evercreech Junction to see the Stephenson Locomotive Society go through. 80043 and 48706 took water amidst soaring profits for Kodak, Ilford and Agfa but the sadder family note was the sight of Evercreech Junction North signalbox burnt out in the mystery fire of the night before. By 7th March the local media were reporting complaints about the replacement bus services.

By 1970 I was living in South Wales. Train journeys to Taunton gave me a chance to see the spoil trains for the M5 Motorway, two Class 37 diesels hauling materials for embankments, some of which were unloading from a special siding alongside the Bason Bridge line. Were these the heaviest trains ever to work that section of the S&D?

In April 1972 I visited Burnham and then walked to Highbridge. The excursion platform still stood at Burnham but the rest of the site was being cleared and along the walk various former access points to the old line were fenced off as development continued. The spoil siding was severed although its embankment completely obliterated the old Works site and the realigned section to Bason Bridge snaked through the former station area. I was in time to see Class 31 Diesel 5824 depart propelling seven milk tanks (the line was now officially a siding) towards the milk factory. That was the last train movement I saw on the Somerset and Dorset.

1978 came along and I was back in Somerset and between jobs. Having joined the Somerset and Dorset Railway Museum Trust (as it then was) I began doing some manning of the Washford Museum, a habit that stuck with me for most of the next 15 years. During that time I talked S&D to hundreds of visitors, made a lot of good friends amongst a group of volunteers who largely kept the family atmosphere of the S&D very much alive and watched the Museum develop. From 1987 onwards there was the regular sight of 53808 at work. One of two surviving members of the 7F 2-8-0 freight locos built specially for the S&D, she maintained the traditions of the class, plodding along day-in, day-out with whatever load the traffic department of the West Somerset Railway asked her to pull. Watching and hearing the 2-8-0 curving round the last 1 in 65 section of the climb from Blue Anchor and running into Washford was very evocative of holiday trains on the S&D in the 1950s. One day in the late '80s a holidaymaker called Hammond paid his admission and got talking to myself and Roy and Mona Pitman as the station dog Sooty kept his eye on us. The visitor seemed quite enthused ...

The Washford years would make a full story in themselves but come 1993 the British Economic Miracle dropped round and I was restructured on to the dole once more.

Then in 1994 I was offered a job in the Minehead office of the West Somerset Railway and at the time of typing I am still there, making my living from steam railways in the 21st century. As with all railwaymen past, present and future there are bad days when getting out of bed feels a major mistake and others when it is the best job going.

It was also in the early '90s that the last members of the Derbyshire side of the family went to the great pit-head bath in the sky. Clearing the effects I also went to see West Hallam station again. The colliery site was cleared and the spoil tip bulldozed and landscaped, leaving the main Great Northern station building as a fine house in a green field that has completely wiped away the rest of the station. Luckily my memories are augmented by Mark Higginson's wonderful book *The Friargate Line*.

But when I get the chance to watch a train leaving Minehead Station and trailing smoke across the fields on the long straight to Dunster I know that the railway bug is still very active in my veins.

(*above right*) Fireman Tony Rossiter, on the running plate of 0-6-0 No.3206, and driver Maurice Cook have their photo taken at Highbridge. (*Maurice Cook collection*)

(*above left*) Fireman Robin Gould, with a cheery smile on top of the Collett tender, as the engine takes on water at Highbridge. (*Alan Mitchard*)

(*left*) Guard Ted Christopher looks very dapper as he leaves for work. Note the lamp in his hand and who is the young child? (*Mrs. M. Brown collection*)

(*right*) Driver Walt Jeans, on the left, with fireman Dave Young, carrying his trusty tea can, are seen here at Highbridge loco cabin. (*Dave Young collection*)

(*left*) Fireman Keith Conibeer beside 3F No.43201 with a fully laden tender at Highbridge, about to work back down the branch. (*Keith Conibeer collection*)

(*right*) The last day at Highbridge with Ivatt Tank No.41283 the leading locomotive on the RCTS special. Note the whitewashed buffers, spotless headlamps, clean smokebox, with wreath upon the front and the white coupling and lamp brackets, all a symbol of the pride the S&D men took in their work. The driver on the right is Fritz Lawrence with fireman Dennis Nettley in the cab. (*David Walden*)

(*above*) GWR Collett 0-6-0 No.3210 prepares to leave Highbridge ahead of the LCGB special, The Somerset & Dorset Rail Tour on 30 September 1962. (*Keith Barrett collection*)

(*right*) Driver Maurice Cook looks out of the cab of Ivatt 2-6-2T No.41307 as he is about to go on to the turntable at Highbridge. (*Maurice Cook collection*)

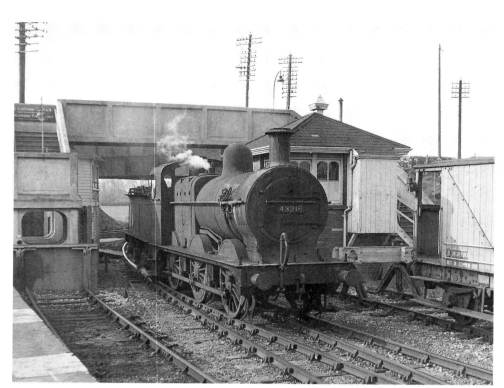

(*left*) A regular sight at Highbridge, as a Bulldog 3F No.43216 is leaving the WR line for the S&D. (*John Cornelius*)

(*right*) 3F No.43216 returns to S&D territory after completing the freight transfer shunt at Highbridge. (*John Cornelius*)

(*below*) Driver Maurice Cook glances towards the photographer as he shunts class 2251 No.2277 across the WR mainline at Highbridge on 28 April 1962. (*John Cornelius*)

The tranquillity of Burnham-on-Sea station, as 3F No.43682 is about to set off with a train for Templecombe. (*Brian Harding*)

(*above*) 2-4-0 No.16A, previously No.20, built by Vulcan Foundry in 1866, is seen here at Burnham-on-Sea about to pull out with a passenger train in 1906. This elderly lady was retired in 1914. Note the small signalbox on the edge of the platform. (*Richard Dagger collection*)

(*below*) Another smashing photograph, taken from the roadway, of 3F No.43682 standing on the foot crossing to the excursion platform at Burnham-on-Sea in 1961. (*Peter Barnfield*)

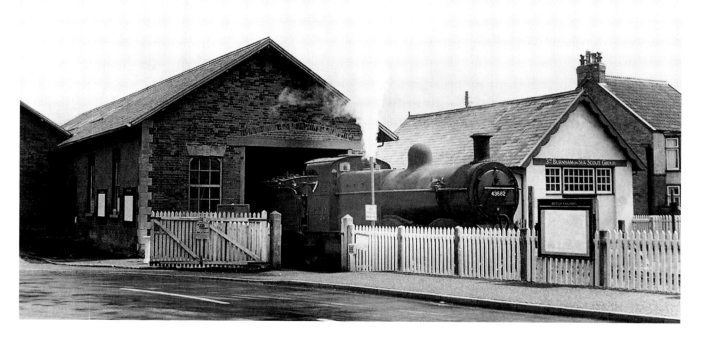

Shunting in the Wells Priory Road sidings is Ivatt class 2MT No.46527. This loco was the last to be built in its class. (*Keith Barrett collection*)

Wells Priory Road, with an S&D train from Glastonbury waiting on the left, headed by Johnson 1P No.1278. Running in from Tucker Street is a GWR 2-6-2T on a local train. (*Keith Barrett collection*)

Looking over the fence in 1949 at Polsham station, facing towards Wells. In the 40s and 50s Stan Ford and his wife looked after the crossing. Stan was also the railway lorry driver delivering parcels around Wells. Now Stan liked his drink and when calling at farms that brewed home-made scrumpy, he would be invited to sample a cup. The chief goods clerk, being suspicious of Stan's activities, decided to go out with him. Stan took him out on more calls than usual that day and declined the kind invitation of the farmers' cups of scrumpy. The chief clerk, not knowing the strength of the brew, accepted their kind offers. When they returned to Wells the chief clerk fell out of the lorry and crawled home, never to bother Stan again. (*Joe Moss/R.S. Carpenter collection*)

(*above*) The hay cart on the former trackbed adds a nice touch to the setting of Cossington station taken in 1964, 12 years after closure to passenger traffic. (*Author's collection*)

(*below*) A rare photograph taken at Bawdrip Halt in 1952, with the 10.10 Edington to Bridgwater train, pulled by an unidentified 3F Bulldog. (*Will Locke collection*)

Horse and carts are the order of the day as staff at Bridgwater station pose for their photograph, c.1890s. On the left of the picture is a notice board with the heading London & South Western Railway. (*SDRT collection*)

(*above*) A wonderful old picture of Hodge's Railway Hotel in Bridgwater, by the GWR station. This was the setting on 1 December 1851 for a meeting of promoters for the purpose of constructing a railway line from Highbridge to Glastonbury (see Robin Atthill's book *The Somerset & Dorset Railway*). The hotel at the time was owned by William Hodge. (*Michael Hodge collection*)

(*left*) Bridgwater North station between 1892 and 1910. The group on the platform, beside the guard on the right, may be the Tully family of Shapwick. (*SDRT collection*)

Dennis Ashill

As a boy I can remember going to see my father at Bridgwater North yard and getting a ride on the footplate of the engine when it ran round with the coaches. The locos would be anything from a Johnson Tank to a 3F. Some of the crews I recall were George Yard, Norman Cook, Bill May, George Brooks and Stan Bedford.

My father, Gilbert Ashill, started on the S&D at Bridgwater in 1910 as a porter and later a carter. He served in the Royal Engineers during the First World War as a wagon driver. On his return he went back to the S&D. During the 1920s he was a lorry driver making deliveries and collecting goods from around the rural areas. He was a well-known character around Bridgwater, probably for his fondness of a jar of cider. He was often greeted by his workmates with 'Got the jar, Gil'. Cider seemed to be drunk at all times during the day and it was not unusual to find a jar in the yard work hut.

One story my father told me was about a horse-drawn railway vehicle when the drayman went into the pub near Bridgwater station and got very drunk. The men in the pub put the drayman on the cart, the horse knew the route and took the cart back to the yard, much to the amazement of the staff. On another occasion one of the draymen set out with a load and after calling at the village pub, brought most of the goods back. It was said that he couldn't remember why he did this – of course it had nothing to do with the amount of cider he had consumed.

Another story was about an old driver who had had his fair share of the apple juice. He took a train out from Bridgwater to Edington. The fireman, seeing he had more than enough, took over the driving and on arriving at Edington one of the porters laid him on a sack barrow and wheeled him home to Burtle.

During the apple-picking season Dad would collect barrels of apples from outlying farms and quite often would be given a glass of cider as refreshment. I often wondered how he managed to drive his lorry back to the yard without mishap, sometimes in the dark on winding, narrow country roads.

In the 1940s he was involved in a road accident whilst cycling home and was left with a badly damaged leg. He was unable to drive his lorry again and once more became a goods porter and later a cranes man, which brought him into contact with the well-liked Cyril (Captain) Burrows who travelled around maintaining the cranes on the branch. Cyril remembers how proud S&D men were about working on the railway and recalls how upset driver Charlie King was when he was five months short of receiving his service watch. To qualify you had to do 45 years. Cyril has memories of a derailment where some coal wagons broke away at Pylle. Working with the breakdown gang of Reg Denning, Phil Owen, Larry Storey and others, they were each paid £2 for the Sunday working. So you certainly didn't work on the S&D for the money.

On another occasion porter Will Locke, a stalwart of Bridgwater North station, remembers a derailment when some goods were being shunted at Cossington. A truck had been left on the main branch while the guard completed his shunt; suddenly it started to move and gather speed before the guard could apply the brake on the slope. The guard phoned Tom Mogg the Edington signalman and told him to expect a runaway truck. The lone truck with speeds of up to 40mph was put in the bay by Tom. It crashed with an almighty bang into the stop blocks. With nobody hurt it was all hushed up and repaired by the gangers, so the guard was spared a grilling by the inspector.

Will also recalls that Bridgwater North had a number of sidings; these consisted of arrival and departure in the station, and four loading sidings including one to a large goods shed. There were two going to a river wharf and another two to a timber merchants. Also there was a shortened length to a cattle pen and one for loading bulk timber. There were also two very short sidings, one to a small Allotment Society Warehouse and one to an engine shed.

All movements to the station and yard were operated by the signalbox where I was later to work, situated by Drove Road Crossing. Just 50 yards away in the direction of Bawdrip, Board's Brickyard had a siding which was operated by hand points. Bridgwater station was once thriving, with lots of industries relying on the railway and a fair amount of passenger traffic. There were also many excursion trains that went from Bridgwater. The brickyards, which employed over six hundred people, would have trips to Blackpool, Southsea and other resorts. You also had hundreds of people using the railway to come to the carnivals, fairs or for shopping.

My father retired in October 1957, but continued to help out in the yard for another year; the railway was his life. I have memories of going into the yard with my father and having a ride in the lorry when delivering goods to shops and factories around the area. Later when my father was working in the yard with foreman Fred Gilbert and porters Sam Farthing and Jerry Jennings, I would see all the mixture of goods being loaded and unloaded. It included bricks from Colthurst and Symons and timber and wicker products from other local factories.

In 1947 I commenced employment at the age of 14 as a boy telephonist in the signalbox at Bridgwater GWR. I did my National Service and after training I went to Longmoor Military Railway as a signalman. On my return, I went to work on the S&D at Bridgwater North as a relief signalman where I was still employed by the Western Region, which then had control of the line. It was with some pleasure and sadness that I went to work where my father Gilbert

had spent most of his working life, in the knowledge that it would only be for a short time. I can remember thinking that the training required to pass out before working the signals was very strict. It took three weeks, during which time I had to travel the line a few times with the inspector and take a written and oral test on the signalling rules and regulations before being allowed to operate the signalbox. I remember a newly qualified signalman had a train ready to leave, but was unable to pull the starting signal off. He told the engine driver it was alright to pass the signal as the line was clear, which he did. Unfortunately as the train started away the engine became derailed at the catch points. The signalman had forgotten to set the points correctly. So you can't get enough training.

During the time I was there I would open up the signalbox to allow the one train a day from Edington Junction. After it had arrived I would assist the guard with the shunting of the train. At times the yard was still quite busy with coal being unloaded and bagged up. At the station I worked with Mrs. Neale who was the clerk, lorry drivers Percy Jubin and Bill Lush, Percy Parsons in the goods shed, Mrs. Nichols the crossing keeper at Horsey Road and of course porters Will Locke and Mr. Duncombe.

In the week before closure I remember the permanent way men laying the connection which joined the old GWR dock line to the S&D to the yard. On the last day they began to change the points operated from the signalbox to locally operated points. It was a very sad day when I gave the train driver the single line token for the very last time and watched the goods train disappear for ever. When it arrived at Edington Junction I received the train out of section signal. I locked up the signalbox and returned the key to the old station booking office. After many years, the Bridgwater Line closed and the site of the station is now a supermarket. That's progress, or is it?

Signalman Dennis Ashill about to leave home for his turn at Bridgwater signalbox. (*Dennis Ashill collection*)

This view of the track and warehousing at Hooper's Yard Bridgwater was taken in 1958. (*Keith Barrett collection*)

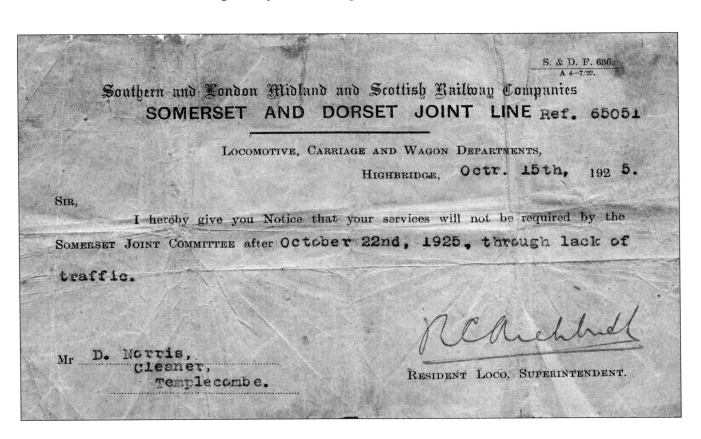

S. & D. F. 636.
A 4—7/22.

Southern and London Midland and Scottish Railway Companies

SOMERSET AND DORSET JOINT LINE Ref. 65051

LOCOMOTIVE, CARRIAGE AND WAGON DEPARTMENTS,

HIGHBRIDGE, Octr. 15th, 192 5.

SIR,

I hereby give you Notice that your services will not be required by the

SOMERSET JOINT COMMITTEE after October 22nd, 1925, through lack of

traffic.

Mr D. Norris,
Cleaner,
Templecombe.

RESIDENT LOCO. SUPERINTENDENT.

Index

Phillips, Ern 61, 62
Pippen, Bill (Gabby) 53, 61, 63
Pitman, George 108
Pitman, Mona 140
Pitman, Roy 140
Pleece, A. 10
Polden, John 76
Pollard, Michael 9
Poole, Emily 39
Poore, Ralph 124
Pothecary, Edgar 10
Prior, Bill 37, 42, 82

Rawlings, Charlie 27, 28
Rawlings, Tom 27
Read, Bert 14
Reakes, Michael 38, 42
Rendle, Dave 76
Reynolds, Howard 39
Rhymes, Bert 118
Rice, Alan 74
Rice, John 133
Richards, Cyril 53
Ridout, Don 99
Ridout, Ivor (Ginger) 105
Riggs, Ernie 53
Robinson, Charlie 76
Rose, Len 76
Rossiter, Tony 139, 141
Routley, Stan 38, 39
Rowett, Arthur 8,10
Russell, Alf 58
Ryall, Mike 39
Ryan, Bob 27, 28

Salisbury, Tom 119
Sanger, Dolly 77
Saunders, Bob 77
Savory, George 100
Savory, Wilf 99
Sawyer, John 39
Scammell, Bert 99
Scovell, Rodney 48, 62, 129
Selman, Arthur 26
Shearn, Ken 29
Sherlock, Bert 99
Shore, Max 39
Silk, Bill 94
Simms, Bet 138
Simms, Edna 138
Simms, Jack 138
Simms, Joe 138
Simms, John 138-140
Simms, Ted 138
Singh, Brian 9

Slocombe, Reg 133
Smith, Sid 38
Smithers, Eric 106
Smithers, Graham 106
Smyth, Walter (Paddy) 58
Snook, Albert 99
Sooty, 140
Southway, Bill 37
Spencer, Richard 100
Stacey, William 38
Staddon, Frank 38, 58
Staddon, Reg 139
Stagg, W. 10
Stamp, John 39
Stokes, Ken 77
Stokes, Nick 76
Stokes, Ray 62, 76, 111
Stoodley, Pete 62
Storey, Larry 155
Stowe, Mr. 10
Strawbridge, David 38-39
Strong, Paul 132
Styling, Frank 76
Summerville, Jock 27
Symes, Dick 37, 42

Tamblyn, Tom 38
Tapper, Jack 27, 28
Target, Bob 77
Taylor, Albert 52
Taylor, Len 72-73
Thick, Fred 53
Toller, Fred 10
Totterdell, Barry 9
Trigg, Bill 60, 62
Tucker, Sam 37
Turner, Raymond 9

Vaughan, Alan 62
Vaughan, Charlie 52, 62

Wagner, Christopher 26
Wake, J. 10
Waldron, Cecil 11
Walker, Johnny 65, 75
Walters, Harry 37, 42
Ware, Bernard 58
Warren, Les 62
Warren, Walt 106
Watkins, Charlie 18
Watts, Bill 77
Webb, Bill 77,83
Webb, Jeremy 80
Webb, John 23,38
Webb, Walter 80, 83, 85

Webber, Eric 39
Webster, Bert 29
Weeks, Dickie 10
Weeks, Walt 27
Welch, George 18, 35, 93, 129
Wescombe, Jack 29
West, Len 17
Wheadon, George 62
Whitaker, Alfred 29
White, Ian 77
White, Tony 75
Whiting, Harold (Nobby) 104
Whitlock, Vic 84
Whittle, Irving 65
Wiffin, Ron 77
Wilds, Bill 10
Williams, George 82
Williams, Jesse 27, 28
Williams, Les 61, 62
Williams, Vic 82, 83
Willoughby, Mr. 27
Willsher, Les 23, 58
Wilson, Allan 10
Wilson, Eric 27, 28, 39
Wiltshire, Bill 10
Wise, Bill 10
Wolley, Harry 10
Wood, Andrew 9
Woods, Walt 23
Wotley, Jack 10
Wright, Jack 80

Yard, George 155
Yelling, Jimmy 52, 62
Young, Dave (Zippo) 62, 141
Young, Tony 29